NONPROFIT ESSENTIALS
The Capital Campaign

Julia Ingraham Walker

WILEY

John Wiley & Sons, Inc.

This book is printed on acid-free paper. ∞

Copyright © 2005 by John Wiley & Sons, Inc. All rights reserved.

Published by John Wiley & Sons, Inc., Hoboken, New Jersey
Published simultaneously in Canada

For general information on our other products and services, or technical support, please contact our Customer Care Department within the United States at 800-762-2974, outside the United States at 317-572-3993 or fax 317-572-4002.

Wiley also publishes its books in a variety of electronic formats. Some content that appears in print may not be available in electronic books.

Library of Congress Cataloging-in-Publication Data:

ISBN 0-471-68429-5

Printed in the United States of America

10 9 8 7 6 5 4 3 2 1

The AFP Fund Development Series

The AFP Fund Development Series is intended to provide fund development professionals and volunteers, including board members (and others interested in the not-for-profit sector), with top-quality publications that help advance philanthropy as voluntary action for the public good. Our goal is to provide practical, timely guidance and information on fund raising, charitable giving, and related subjects. AFP and Wiley each bring to this innovative collaboration unique and important resources that result in a whole greater than the sum of its parts. For information on other books in the series, please visit:

http://www.afpnet.org/tier3_cd.cfm?content_item_id=2584&folder_id=1485

The Association of Fundraising Professionals

The AFP is a professional association of fund-raising executives which advances philanthropy through its more than 26,000 members in over 172 chapters throughout the United States, Canada, and Mexico. Through its advocacy, research, education, and certification programs, the Society fosters development and growth of fundraising professionals, works to advance philanthropy and volunteerism, and promotes high ethical standards in the fundraising profession.

2004-2005 AFP Publishing Advisory Council

Linda L. Chew, CFRE, Chair
Associate Director, Alta Bates Summit Foundation

Nina P. Berkheiser, CFRE
Director of Development, SPCA of Pinellas County

Samuel N. Gough, CFRE
Principal, The AFRAM Group

Robert Mueller, CFRE
*Director of Development, Alliance of Community Hospices &
Palliative Care Services*

Maria Elena Noriega
Director, Noriega Malo & Associates

Audrey P. Kintzi , CFRE
Chief Advancement Officer, Girl Scout Council St. Croix Valley

Danis Prud'homme
Executive Director, Juvenile Diabetes Research Foundation

John Wiley & Sons

Susan McDermott
Editor (Professional/Trade Division), John Wiley & Sons

AFP Staff

Jan Alfieri
Manager, AFP Resource Center, AFP

Walter Sczudlo
*Executive Vice President, Programs and Public Policy &
General Counsel*

Acknowledgments

I have been fortunate to have had many mentors throughout my career; while I can't name them all here, there are a few special people who have helped me to learn and try out the basic principles in this book. Thanks to my old friends from Tulane: Eamon Kelly, Yvette Jones, Pat Mason, and John Martinez; thanks to all the members of my former staff, especially Gail Mast, Beth Turner, Julie Nice, Mireya Castano, and Eva Martinez; and thanks to just a few of the many generous donors who helped me understand what philanthropy really means: Peter Aron, Louis Freeman, Boatner Reily, Paul Spencer, and the late great Jack Aron. I am also grateful to Ned Lees of Marts and Lundy, who taught me about gift tables, and to Florence Andre, for showing me the path to a consulting career.

I would like to thank all of my clients for giving me the chance to learn so much about capital campaigns, especially the talented development people at Newman School, Xavier University, and The National D-Day Museum. Each client has taught me about their own unique needs, and I couldn't have written this without the wonderful experience I gained from working with all of them. Special thanks go to Carol McCall and Eva Martinez for reading parts of this manuscript, as well as to Jan Alfieri and her committee at AFP for selecting me as one of their authors. I also owe a big debt of gratitude to my editor at John Wiley & Sons, Susan McDermott, for so capably guiding me through this process.

And finally, my appreciation goes to my patient husband, Cedric, who served as my information systems specialist, and to my sons, Jake and Ben. Jake read the manuscript and advised me to add some humor, while Ben helped me to remember my favorite development stories. I couldn't have done it without the three of you.

About the Author

Julia Ingraham Walker holds a BA and MA in English from Tulane University and an MBA from Rollins College in Florida. Her initial marketing expertise was formed during 10 years as a professional in college admissions, first at Tulane and then as Director of Admissions at Rollins. In 1985 she returned to New Orleans and began a career in fundraising that has spanned 20 years and numerous positions ranging from annual fund to major gifts.

In 1990 Ms. Walker was appointed Vice President for Institutional Advancement at her alma mater, Tulane, where she served until 1998. In this position she supervised over 100 employees in the advancement area and directed the University's $250 million capital campaign. Tulane's campaign raised over $75 million for endowment as well as providing the resources for construction or major renovation of eight campus buildings. In 1994 Ms. Walker was named Outstanding Fundraising Executive by her peers in the New Orleans chapter of AFP, the Association of Fundraising Professionals.

Ms. Walker has been active as an independent fundraising consultant since 1998 and has conducted and advised campaigns that total over $600 million. Her clients include a wide range of nonprofits, from museums and schools to grass-roots community organizations. She has helped to manage capital campaigns for clients in religion, health care, the arts, historic preservation, low-income housing, K–12 education, universities, and research. Her areas of expertise include campaign feasibility studies, campaign planning and implementation, and nonprofit management, including management and training of nonprofit staff, volunteers, and boards.

Ms. Walker is a member of AFP and has participated in numerous conferences and workshops on fundraising topics. The mother of two sons, Jacob and Benjamin, Ms. Walker is married to Cedric Walker, a Professor of Biomedical Engineering at Tulane University.

Contents

Introduction

All progress is based upon a universal innate desire on the part of every organism to live beyond its income.

—Samuel Butler (1835–1902), *Notebooks*, 1912

Every nonprofit worthy of mention seems to need more money. Designed to meet current operational needs at best, the annual budget of most nonprofits never allows for the level of expansion, enhancement, growth, and new programming that their leaders desire to fulfill the mission of the organization. Capital campaigns are designed to fulfill these needs.

This book is written to help you and your organization achieve success with your capital campaign. From the first days of planning to the last pledge reminder, the "how to's" of the capital campaign are laid out in straightforward, easy to understand steps that any organization can put to good use. This book provides rules, tips, techniques, exhibits, samples, stories, and programs to help you succeed. What it can't provide is the soul of the enterprise: the mission, the vision, the energy, the excitement, and the generosity of thousands of supporters that you will find in your own organization and in your own community.

The spirit of private philanthropy is alive and well in America today. In spite of all the uncertainties of modern life, we are motivated to give by the sense that we can improve and change the world we live in. Private philanthropy underwrites the activities of almost every nonprofit in the country, providing support for initiatives in health care, the arts, education, housing, religion, social services, and community services.

Over the past few decades, our concept of philanthropy has expanded and broadened, moving beyond seeking generous gifts from the wealthy few to tapping the giving power of millions of donors earning average incomes who contribute to charities across the globe. The combined impact of these charitable contributions is enormous:

> American individuals, estates, foundations, and corporations gave an estimated $240.72 billion to charitable causes in 2003. Since 1998, charitable giving has been 2 percent or more of gross domestic product (GDP). For 2003, total contributions are estimated to be 2.2 percent of GDP.[1]

Given the $241 billion donated annually, it is not surprising that nonprofit boards and executive directors have come to view fundraising as crucial to the progress of their institutions. Goals and expectations for fundraising have increased dramatically. In response, the sophistication of the advancement office at both the operational and management levels has also improved markedly to meet these challenges.

Nowhere is that increased level of sophistication more apparent than in the expanded use of the capital campaign in nonprofit fundraising. The successful capital campaign is more than the sum of its parts. Beyond just raising more money, the capital campaign can help the institution define its priorities, cele-

---

[1] Giving USA Foundation, a public service initiative of the Trust for Philanthropy of the American Association of Fundraising Counsel (AAFRC).

brate its vision, and bring together its diverse constituents as they work together in a meaningful endeavor.

The capital campaign is one of the most sophisticated, complex activities that a nonprofit organization can undertake. Every campaign develops a life of its own. It builds momentum toward success, or dies on the vine, based on a set of subtle but identifiable characteristics. It tests the mettle of the entire nonprofit team: volunteers, executive directors, board members, staff members, and supporters.

This book will help you get started and keep you on the track toward achieving your organization's larger goals. The capital campaign can help launch your organization to reach new heights, build new buildings, create new programs, and secure its financial future. Take a deep breath, keep focused, and enjoy the ride—your capital campaign is about to begin.

We make a living by what we get, we make a life by what we give.

—Sir Winston Churchill

CHAPTER 1

Before Beginning Your Capital Campaign

 After reading this chapter, you will be able to:

- Understand the goals and objectives of capital campaigns.
- Evaluate your organization's readiness for a campaign.
- Define your organization's needs.

Goals and Objectives of the Capital Campaign

Capital campaigns have become a fixture in the nonprofit world. From small campaigns that raise thousands of dollars for grassroots community service organizations to the huge, billion-dollar efforts mounted by the nation's premiere universities, campaigns and all their accompanying activity have become a prominent part of the landscape for charitable organizations and their leaders.

Some nonprofit leaders consider them a necessary evil. Others revel in the opportunity that a campaign presents to share the mission of their organization more broadly with constituents, both new and old. Many find that a capital campaign brings together all their various stakeholders as they work to meet a common goal. Planned and executed well, a capital campaign can truly energize a nonprofit organization, having an impact far beyond the raising of funds.

What Is a Capital Campaign?

A capital campaign is a set of fundraising and outreach activities that are focused on raising money for a specific, defined need (or set of needs) beyond annual operating funds for a nonprofit organization. Most capital campaigns have as their goal the construction or renovation of a building or facility. The word *capital* signifies an expenditure of a nonrecurring nature, such as funds spent on physical plant, equipment, or property.

In many capital campaigns today, however, the term is defined fairly loosely, and funds are raised for capital, endowment, program, and operations all at once. Some campaigns raise money for a new building, but include funds for other expenses the building will incur, such as furnishings, landscaping, equipment, exhibits, and technology support. Capital campaigns can also be used to seek funds to pay staff, support programs, and cover ongoing maintenance costs for a new facility. It has become more common in recent years for campaigns to help secure the long-term financial health of the organization by including an endowment component.

While a nonprofit may be unique in the exact components, timetable, and goals of its campaign, there are overall similarities to campaigns that transcend organizational differences. Most capital campaigns share certain characteristics:

- An identified set of needs that determines the purpose of the campaign

- A defined financial goal that determines the size of the campaign

- A set timetable for meeting the goal, usually longer than one year

- An identified group of volunteers who help conduct fundraising activity

- A focus on raising major gifts, that is, gifts that are larger than the normal annual fund support that the organization receives

- A plan for public recognition of donors who make major gifts, which could vary from the naming of spaces in a new building to engraving a donor wall

While these shared characteristics help define most campaigns, there are several different types of campaigns to consider when you begin your campaign planning. Types of campaigns are usually defined by the purpose or use of the funds raised (see Exhibit 1.1). A comprehensive capital campaign, for instance, would combine fundraising for a capital project with all types of funds the organization needed over a set period of time, including funds raised for annual operations, programmatic support, and endowment.

TIPS & TECHNIQUES

What Type of Campaign Does Your Organization Need? Consider the Following Factors:

- The type of funding your organization needs most

- The capability within your organization to plan and implement a complex campaign with multiple goals

- Your organization's need for and ability to manage endowment funds

- The size and financial capability of your organization's prospect pool

- Staffing and volunteer resources that will be available for your efforts

- Prior campaign experience in your organization

The prior fundraising experience of your organization is an important consideration in selecting the type of campaign you will mount. If you have just completed a major campaign for a new facility, you may want to consider building your endowment or setting a smaller goal with minicampaigns for projects that still need funding.

If your organization has never done a capital campaign, it is preferable to keep things simple and focus just on the capital needs for one new facility. If your organization has campaign experience, and has the resources to keep lots

---

EXHIBIT 1.1

Types of Campaigns:
Defined by Purpose of the Funds Raised

Capital: Funds raised for a new or renovated facility. May include funding for expenses related to the facility, such as furnishings, equipment, program, staffing, exhibits, technology, and maintenance.

Endowment: Funds raised for the organization's endowment, that is, funds where the principal is invested and only the interest is spent on the use specified by the donor. May be combined with a capital campaign.

Annual: Funds raised for annual ongoing operations expenses. May be combined with a capital campaign.

Comprehensive: Includes all types of funds raised for the organization during a defined time period, including annual fund, endowment, program, and capital.

Minicampaigns: A group of small, focused projects that are marketed together as in a capital campaign, used for funding a set of identified needs in one organization.

of fundraising projects moving at once, then you may be better served by pulling all your needs together and mounting a comprehensive campaign.

Improving Fundraising Results

Most institutions find that capital campaigns help them to improve fundraising results, even after the campaign goals have been met. This is because a campaign tends to encourage more giving across the institution for all purposes. The combined effect of the additional attention to marketing, the time and focus on fundraising by senior staff and the president, the increase in volunteer fundraising activity, and the outreach to new prospects usually results in bringing in more money in larger increments from more donors.

Many campaign advisers measure nonprofit fundraising by the *run rate*, or the amount of cash raised each year from all sources for all purposes. Campaigns tend to affect the run rate positively. It is common, for instance, to see a campaign double the run rate for an institution; some increase by an even larger percentage. With careful planning and maintenance of campaign levels of budget and staffing, much of this increase in the run rate can be sustained beyond the campaign.

A related goal for the capital campaign in organizational terms is to improve overall fundraising capability on a long-term basis. Some foundations will make "capacity building" grants that support campaign staffing and expenditures for this reason: as the old story goes, if you *teach* a man to fish, it is better for him in the long run than if you *give* the man a fish. If a nonprofit learns how to effectively fundraise, and the expertise of its president, its board, its volunteer base, and its advancement staff all improve during the campaign period, then the nonprofit will finish the campaign better able to meet its needs in the future.

Because campaigns tend to improve fundraising results for both the short term and long term, they are popular with nonprofit leaders and board members who want to see their organizations build fundraising momentum and succeed in meeting aggressive funding goals.

It's Not Just About Money: Setting Other Goals

There are other reasons to mount a campaign, however, than simply raising more money. First, the campaign brings a wide variety of people together to work on achieving a unified goal. This can be a galvanizing experience within a nonprofit for staff, leadership, and volunteers. Like the military and political campaign, the capital campaign requires tremendous logistical support: the hiring, training, and deploying of staff and volunteers ultimately will determine the level of success that can be achieved. It is partly the process, the coming together of disparate parts and people both inside and outside of the organization to achieve a common goal, that makes it such a valuable experience.

Another goal that can be achieved during the campaign is to reach out to new constituencies. Because of the enhanced marketing and fundraising efforts that are put in place to support the campaign, new friends are made for the nonprofit. With forethought and targeted marketing, the organization can broaden its base of supporters. It may want to attract more national donors, or more women donors, or build support in minority communities for its mission. Using the campaign to broaden the base of support for the nonprofit allows for future growth and support from a wider variety of donors, which ultimately strengthens the organization.

Finally, the campaign can help an organization focus on the big picture—its mission and vision. It takes a clear and compelling message to attract donors

RULES OF THE ROAD

Don't sell a space that keeps disappearing from the plans.

and financial support to a campaign. Nonprofit leaders must create a vision of the future of the organization that forms the core of that compelling message. The process of communicating the organization's needs—sharing the vision with those who are being asked to provide support—enhances the understanding and commitment of all those connected to the organization.

Another way to describe this effect is that in communicating what is important about the organization to new supporters, the leaders of the organization reaffirm their own commitment to the organization's mission. Thus at the end of a successful campaign, the organization has a cadre of trained, articulate leaders who share a similar perspective about the vision for the organization's future direction. This can be a very powerful experience that creates a group of dedicated leaders who can continue to move the organization forward.

Are You Ready for a Capital Campaign?

Preparing for a capital campaign is no small matter. Depending on the size and complexity of your campaign, it can take months or years of preparation before a single dollar is raised.

Most importantly, the organization has to have strong leadership in place to mount a capital campaign. For a nonprofit organization to succeed in a major campaign, the institutional leaders (the president and the senior staff, especially the heads of operations, finance, and development) need to be smart, skilled, and work well together as a team. Additionally, a campaign requires strong volunteer leadership from the board and campaign chairs to focus on their own philanthropy and reach out to prospective donors.

A capital campaign requires broad agreement across the institution on the campaign needs, a financial goal to meet those needs, and a pricing structure for naming opportunities. There are preparatory steps that focus on internal issues, such as augmenting staff, budget, infrastructure, and program support.

There is also preparation required for external elements, such as donor identi-fication, institutional PR, and creating the case for support that will be used to approach prospective donors.

Leadership Assessment

How can you determine if your organization is ready to mount a capital cam-paign? Start with a leadership assessment, since good leadership is essential to the campaign's ultimate success. There are three critical points to assess in terms of organizational leadership: the president or executive director, the board, and the campaign volunteer leadership.

Evaluating the current and potential leadership of the organization should be viewed as an opportunity to strengthen the overall organization and to shore up weaknesses, not as a threat. A leadership assessment can be made informally by the executive director (including a self-assessment), it can be conducted by the president and the board chair working together, or it can be made with the aid of an outside consultant. The goal is to uncover and address leadership gaps or problems and correct them before the pressures of the cam-paign make adjustments more difficult.

Leadership Assessment of the President or Executive Director. The nonprofit CEO will have to commit a substantial percentage of her time, energy, and focus to the campaign for it to be successful. Some presidents feel that they can delegate fundraising duties to staff or volunteers, but top donors almost always require personal attention from the top executive in order to make a leadership gift. Many executive directors spend as much as one-half to two-thirds of their time fundraising during a capital campaign. Due to this high time commitment, CEOs should plan to delegate a portion of their other executive duties to their senior staff. Planning for this hand-off should take place before the campaign begins.

Questions to Ask in Assessing the President/Executive Director:

- *Is she a good fundraiser?* If not, she should enroll in some training seminars or work with a mentor to build her skills before the campaign starts.

- *Does she work well with the board?* Good communication between board leadership and the executive director is important to keep the campaign running smoothly. Address communication and governance problems before the campaign gets underway.

- *Is she planning on staying for the duration of the campaign?* A change in mid-campaign can put off donors, prospects, and board members who have invested time and energy into their relationship with the president. Make sure contract renewal dates match the campaign timetable.

- *Is there a change at the top being considered?* If there is a perception that the leader is weak or ineffective, make the change before the campaign is begun, or the campaign effort will lose valuable time and momentum.

- *Are there functions she can delegate to senior staff to clear her time for campaign activity?* The executive director will be directly involved in much campaign activity. Her ability to delegate other functions effectively will depend on her management skills and the strength of her senior management team.

If the executive director is new or inexperienced in fundraising, it is especially important to help her develop those skills before the pressures of a campaign bear down. There are numerous workshops and training programs now offered for executives; professional groups such as the Association of Fundraising Professionals (AFP) and the Council for Advancement and Support of Education (CASE) offer special programs targeted at senior non-profit executives. There are also seminars where presidents and board members can attend in teams and learn to work together to improve their skills.

Leadership Assessment of the Board. Many organizations use the planning time before a major campaign as a period during which they undertake a formal review of board governance and membership. Campaigns flourish or wilt depending on the strength of their organization's board. The period before a campaign begins is the best time to add new members, increase diversity, improve geographic representation, and increase the number of members.

Questions to Ask in Assessing the Board:

- *Is the board chair prepared for the campaign?* The board chair often serves as the "face" of the organization in the broader community; is he prepared to play that role? Can he make fundraising calls on key prospects? Perhaps additional training in fundraising or media relations should be provided. Is the next chairperson identified and being trained?

- *Is the board capable of giving a substantial portion of the campaign goal?* Many boards contribute between 30 and 50% of the campaign goal; does your board have enough members who can make leadership gifts?

- *Are there board members who have fundraising expertise?* While you may have a separate Capital Campaign Committee, many board members also cultivate and solicit campaign gifts. Are your board members ready to do this effectively?

- *Has the board "bought into" the reasons for the campaign?* The board must be fully engaged in the campaign, so that they will make their own gifts and bring others into the fold. They should be educated about the needs for the campaign and excited about where the organization is headed.

- *Is the board big enough and diverse enough to take on this campaign?* Some boards may need to expand in size to increase their reach into different areas of the community. Expanding geographic representation, racial and ethnic diversity, and having board members who represent different industry segments can add depth and new capabilities to the board before a campaign begins.

It is appropriate to make sure that there are members who have access to money and influence in your community (or nationwide) on your board before the campaign begins. Board members are chosen for many reasons, including the knowledge and commitment that they bring to your mission and services, but it is also important to have some board members with the capacity to make large gifts or who have access to those who can make gifts. It can be awkward to add influential donors to the board during a campaign or immediately after they have made a large gift, so timing is critical in this consideration. The time to add them is *before* the campaign starts.

Leadership Assessment of Potential Campaign Volunteers. A campaign needs good volunteer leadership to be successful, and the ability to identify and recruit the right chair is an important consideration for your campaign. The best volunteer leaders drive the momentum of the campaign, push the staff and other volunteers to keep activity going, undertake key solicitations, and make their own leadership gifts. They keep everyone focused on what needs to be done next. The right leader can make a huge difference in a campaign's chances for success.

Depending on the size of your campaign and of your volunteer base, you may need only one volunteer who can chair the campaign, or you may want to create a network of committees with co-chairs who support regional campaign activity. No matter what form your campaign will take, a core group of volunteer leaders—at least one, but preferably five or six—is needed to lead the activity and keep everyone else moving in a positive direction.

Questions to Ask in Assessing the Campaign Volunteer Leadership:

- *Who is the best person available to chair (or co-chair) the campaign?* The chair needs to be a skilled fundraiser, have a name that is widely respected, and be committed to your cause. Being able to give a lead gift is also a nice plus.

- *Is he or she available and willing to take on this job?* The best chair is often the busiest; time the start of your campaign to take advantage of the availability of your proposed chairperson.

- *What do we need to do to recruit this individual?* Get your board chair involved in this discussion. You may need to be flexible on some issues, such as providing a co-chair, staffing support, or term limits in order to attract your first choice.

- *Do we have five or six other individuals we can count on as volunteer leaders?* Look for potential leaders who can tap corporations or foundations, not just individuals; plan for national or regional representation; select varied occupations and industry representation when assessing your campaign leadership team.

- *Do we need to provide additional training?* Most volunteers need additional training in fundraising techniques, especially planned giving, but they all need to be educated about your organization and needs.

- *Do we need to find additional people?* Identify and recruit potential volunteer leaders well ahead of the scheduled campaign start. Plan for diversity in your volunteer leadership to provide access to all segments of your community.

Inside the Organization

It is a common mistake to assume that only the development office will be affected by a major fundraising campaign. In reality, every operational division—from finance to physical plant—will be profoundly affected by the ongoing demands and ultimate success or failure of the campaign.

The skills and capabilities of your senior management team will help to determine the success of the capital campaign. Identify the senior managers, most likely members of the senior staff or vice presidents, who will help lead the planning and implementation of the campaign in their areas. Shore up any weaknesses in the team, particularly in finance and development. A campaign ultimately is about money, and the people who raise, process, account for, and spend the money have to be first-rate to make it all work.

Do your financial planning ahead of the campaign. Determine if your organization will need to borrow money or sell bonds to support the construction phase if you are doing a capital project. There is often a period between the start of construction and the payment of campaign pledges that requires some type of financing alternative. Consider ways to pay for your campaign expenses (see Chapter 2). Determine the impact of additional expenses of a new facility or program on your operational budget and how that will be covered after the campaign is over.

Consider having a retreat before the campaign starts, led by the executive director with the senior staff present, to discuss the implications of the campaign for staffing, strategic planning, utilization of resources, and financial projections. If a construction project is planned, it is important to plan ahead for project management, and to decide which department head will undertake the oversight of the architectural design, construction, and budget expenditures for the planned facility.

Here are five functional areas inside the organization that should be ready to perform at a high level during the campaign:

1. *Finance:* Provide accurate gift accounting, select and oversee investment managers for the endowment, assist in preparing campaign budget and how to pay for it, and provide financial planning for capital project development.

2. *Advancement:* Hire or train staff to cover campaign-related functions, including prospect research, prospect management, gift processing, proposal writing, event planning, and volunteer management and support. Hire or train staff to gain major gift cultivation and solicitation expertise.

3. *Capital project management:* Identify or hire staff to oversee the architectural design and construction process, maintain budget and quality con-

trol on all contractors, and ensure that project will open on time and on budget.

4. *Operations:* Lead planning for bringing new facility and programs online, plan staffing and program needs for new facility, prepare to track and measure service outcomes, and improve quality of services rendered.

5. *PR/marketing:* Promote overall name recognition for the organization, develop the campaign case (the messages and themes used with prospective donors), and prepare campaign materials and supporting brochures.

Outside the Organization

A capital campaign is essentially a coordinated marketing effort that seeks to heighten interest, awareness, and support for the nonprofit in order to raise funds for a specific purpose or set of needs. Often marketing or feasibility studies are done to measure the support that an organization can expect to receive during the campaign. These studies are reviewed in more detail in Chapter 2. Even before a study is scheduled, however, much work can be done to assess and prepare external audiences for the campaign to come.

Here are steps you can take outside the organization to help prepare for a campaign:

1. *Study the environment for fundraising in your area.* Familiarize yourself with local, regional, and national fundraising trends by joining groups like AFP, talking to your peers, and reading publications such as *The Chronicle of Philanthropy, The Wall Street Journal, and* local business newspapers. Look for factors that might affect your campaign, including: gains and losses in the stock market; regional economic growth or decline; local businesses merging with national conglomerates; the activity of local foundations; and new "hot button" social issues in your community.

2. *Become familiar with what your peers are doing.* Study the capital campaigns of your competitors. Visit their Web sites, review their materials, and talk

to their advancement staff. Don't copy exactly what they are doing, but look for things they do well that might work in your campaign, including: the pricing of naming opportunities; their volunteer structure; the size of their staff and budget; their campaign themes; and the size of their goal.

3. *Analyze your current donor pool.* You should know everything possible about your donor pool before you begin to plan your campaign: how many donors you have at what levels; who the top donors are by name; geographic areas of strength; new areas that show growth potential; and if possible, age, sex, and other demographic information about your donors. This will be used to help you plan your target markets.

4. *Identify target markets you want to focus on.* Take the information from analyzing your donor pool; identify 8 to 10 top cities, regions, or neighborhoods (in a local campaign) that have performed well for your organization in fundraising over the past five years. Then add 4 or 5 cities, regions, or neighborhoods that show growth potential (i.e., there has been some new donor activity there in the past 18 months). These areas will be your target markets.

5. *Begin PR efforts to raise awareness of the organization in target markets.* Now focus your PR efforts on these target cities or neighborhoods. Create a plan with your PR staff to feature stories or publicity about individuals from these areas, begin a concerted effort to get the name of your organization in front of the media outlets in these areas, and begin to identify key volunteers who could help promote your campaign in these cities or regions.

Defining the Organization's Needs

Strategic Planning and the Campaign

In many nonprofit organizations, a capital campaign is the end result of an institutional strategic planning process. The concept behind strategic planning

LIVE & LEARN

During a luncheon at the university president's home, the advancement VP was seated next to a couple whose daughter had just enrolled at the school. The husband was a billionaire whose assets were derived from an international network of businesses including real estate, insurance, and banking. The wife, a lovely Asian woman whose English was a little weak, turned to the VP and politely asked: "And what do you do?" The VP replied, "I am the Vice President for Development." "How nice!" cried the wife. "Development—that's exactly what my husband does."

is to bring together all the stakeholders in the organization through a discussion of future needs across the institution. Most planners now look at a planning horizon of no longer than three to five years, due to the rapid changes in environmental, political, and social factors that influence the future of many of our nonprofits. A longer planning horizon is necessary in nonprofits where long-term financial planning, such as debt service, is a key factor in capital construction.

Undertaking an effective strategic planning exercise allows the organization to prioritize its needs and to create a set of funding priorities. Planning doesn't have to be vague or open ended; it can be focused on desired outcomes. For instance, to prepare for a capital campaign, a hospital might hire an architect, establish a facility master plan, develop space-use policies, and set up a process for determining the best use of limited resources, such as contiguous open land. Once these processes are in place, then projects and priorities can be determined, ultimately with the approval of the board.

While it can deliver valuable results, institution-wide strategic planning can be complex and time consuming. It can also be expensive if you use outside consultants to manage the process. One alternative is to conduct a smaller, more focused planning process internally using the organization's senior management team. To build consensus, it is important to take the results of an internal plan to the board and other external advisory groups for their input and involvement. It is critical to achieve buy-in across the organization, from senior management to the board, before going out to convince donors that they should invest in your plan.

 IN THE REAL WORLD

Leading a
Strategic Planning Process

Here Is the Planning Process That One Nonprofit Followed to Prepare for Its Capital Campaign, Working with Internal Staff:

- Plan for a three-year horizon.
- Identify all potential funding sources (private, public, and internal).
- Look at sources and uses of new funds.
- Develop a cash-flow plan for pledges.
- Brainstorm needs and prioritize projects.
- Distinguish projects from programs.
- Develop plans to staff and operate any new programs or facilities.
- Open up internal communications.
- Develop a theme.
- Construct two or three messages around the theme.
- Create a Table of Needs.
- Separate out endowment needs.

The strategic planning process results in setting the goals for the organization's future and prioritizes the steps toward achieving those goals. Most importantly, however, it brings together different members of the organization's various constituencies, whether they are staff, board members, volunteers, or customers, to work through differences of opinion in an open and positive manner. A good planning process results in a unified vision for the nonprofit's future direction. Lack of planning, or a poor planning process, can result in divisiveness and negativity that distracts an institution and slows its progress.

Preparing the Table of Needs

The Table of Needs is the name given to the list of projects that will be funded through the capital campaign (see Exhibits 1.2 and 1.3). It usually includes a list of the recognition opportunities and prices for naming each component of the project. A Table of Needs is often published as part of the campaign case statement, but since prices and availability can change as the campaign progresses, many organizations print the Table of Needs separately and add it to brochures, proposals, and solicitation packages.

There are three main steps to creating a Table of Needs for your campaign:

1. *Determine the scope of the project you need to raise money for.* Will you build a new facility or renovate an old one? What are your staffing, program, and operating costs going to be? Do you wish to include an endowment component for future operating costs? Do you already own the land for your new building?

2. *Hire an architect or program designer to draw up preliminary plans.* In order to create your Table of Needs, you will need cost estimates for all the project components, an available site, and preliminary design drawings to determine what spaces in the facility can be named for recognition purposes.

3. *Work with the architect to identify and price the most attractive components of the project to offer for recognition to donors.* The price you will list for a space does not have to equate exactly with the cost to construct that space. Use

your most attractive spaces—external naming opportunities, entrance areas, soaring atriums, impressive conference rooms—for the highest-priced options. Then divide up the remaining costs and apply them to rooms of lesser value. It is useful to have all the gifts add up to more than your total campaign in case you don't sell every option.

While there are no standard pricing guidelines for capital campaigns, the external naming price for a building is often set at 30 to 50% of the total cost

---

EXHIBIT 1.2

Sample Table of Needs

$60 Million Capital Campaign for a National Museum:

New Wing (external name)	$ 20 million
Preservation Center	$ 10 million
Theater	$ 10 million
Library/Archives	$ 5 million
Conference Center	$ 5 million
Exhibit Floor I	$ 4 million
Exhibit Floor II	$ 3 million
Exhibit Floor III	$ 2 million
Education Center	$ 1 million
Classrooms	$ 100,000 each
Conference Room	$ 500,000
Galleries	$ 250,000 each
Exhibits	$ 100,000 each
Walkways	$ 50,000 each

EXHIBIT 1.3

Sample Table of Needs

**$1.5 Million Capital Campaign for a Community Arts Center
(includes staffing, program, and endowment):**

New Building (external name)	$ 500,000
Lobby	$ 100,000
Exhibition Hall	$ 250,000
Classrooms (4 @ $25,000 each)	$ 100,000
Conference Room	$ 100,000
Director's Suite	$ 50,000
Staff Director (4 years @ $50,000/yr)	$ 200,000
Education Program	$ 100,000
(can be divided into smaller grants)	
Endowment	$ 250,000
(can be divided into smaller gifts)	

of the project. For example, in a campaign for a facility with a $3 million goal, the external naming gift might be set at $1 million to $1.5 million. (For more on gift pricing to motivate donors, see Chapter 7.)

Test your price list, or Table of Needs, among friendly donors or board members to see if it feels right to them. Sometimes prices can seem too high for a local or regional audience and need to be adjusted downward. In general, campaigns in the northeastern United States and on the west coast can command slightly higher naming prices than those in other regions of the country.

Planning for Bricks-and-Mortar Projects

Most capital campaigns raise funds for either the renovation of an old facility or the construction of a new one. Some campaigns involve multiple buildings, wings, and complex interior designs. All these projects involve substantial architectural planning and interior design. How well you work with your organization's architects and designers will help to determine the ease with which you meet your campaign's goals.

The advancement team needs to keep in close contact with the architect and project planners during the early phases of planning a capital project. This is to allow those who will be doing the fundraising access to detailed information about the project, from room size to the placement of donor recognition plaques. Better information allows the advancement professionals the ability to work more closely with donors to ensure their satisfaction as the project funding progresses.

Architects and designers can become important members of the campaign fundraising team. Architects help support the fundraising process by providing renderings, floor plans, and full-color drawings for visits with donors. These drawings can be personalized to reflect the name of the prospect on the space being pictured. Renderings can be produced electronically and dropped into publications, newsletters, PowerPoint presentations, and CD-ROMs. Architectural drawings are also used in media presentations and packages.

If an architect is eloquent about the purpose and design of a new facility, he can play a major role in building the enthusiasm and excitement that is an integral part of a capital campaign. He may be willing to serve as a presenter at campaign events, including donor visits, prospect cultivation dinners, and campaign kick-off events. In a bricks-and-mortar campaign, the building is the center of attention, and the architect is the creator of the building. Get him involved in the campaign if he will be useful in the fundraising effort.

TIPS & TECHNIQUES

Helpful Hints for Planning Bricks-and-Mortar Projects:

- Get the advancement VP involved early in the architectural planning process and keep her involved.

- Have a member of the advancement team attend regular meetings with the architects and designers to keep abreast of changes.

- Identify one person (not from the advancement staff) as project manager, to oversee contracts, keep the project on budget, select furnishings, and so on.

- Keep tabs on the components listed on the Table of Needs; make sure that they all end up in the project. Don't offer a donor the chance to name a floor that doesn't exist anymore!

- Keep one eye on costs—construction projects often go over budget. The campaign may be asked to raise the additional funds needed on top of its original goal. A good project manager will help to control costs.

Summary

Capital campaigns require substantial planning. Leadership, both inside and outside the organization, is essential to the success of your capital campaign. Assess and deal with any leadership or training issues in your staff and board before launching the campaign. There are many areas of your organization, in addition to the advancement office, that need to make preparations for the campaign. Your organization may find it helpful to conduct a strategic planning exercise before starting your fundraising to map out institutional priorities. Working with an architect and preparing a Table of Needs are additional key steps to help nonprofits prepare for a capital campaign.

CHAPTER 2

Preparing for the Capital Campaign

 After reading this chapter, you will be able to:

- Undertake the campaign planning process.
- Determine if you need a consultant or a feasibility study.
- Plan for campaign budget and staffing needs.

The Campaign Planning Process

Why You Need a Plan

Capital campaigns for nonprofit organizations are among the most complex of civic group endeavors encountered in today's highly networked communities. Like winning a hard-fought election, or playing a competitive team sport, the capital campaign requires careful preparation, extensive teamwork, and skilled execution in order to succeed. A good campaign plan keeps everyone on task and highlights the path toward the campaign's ultimate success.

Developing a campaign plan can meet a number of objectives:

- Build enthusiasm and support for your organization's future needs.

- Harness the energy of those who work and volunteer for your organization.

- Focus everyone's efforts in the same direction.

- Share the organization's mission and vision with new audiences.

- Enhance relationships with donors and prospects.

- Provide the organization's leadership with a blueprint for success.

Who Should Lead the Planning Process?

There are three alternatives for selecting someone to prepare your campaign plan: an internal staff member, a volunteer, or an outside consultant. The best decision for your organization depends on who is available, what skills he or she has, and how much money you have to spend.

Look inside your organization first for an internal staff member who has the knowledge and expertise to write your plan. Having a campaign plan written by a staff member can result in getting the plan completed faster and costs less than hiring a consultant. It also can prove advantageous to use an internal person who is already intimately familiar with the needs, resources, and constituencies of your organization.

Some organizations use their chief development officer or president to prepare the campaign plan; others have a campaign director, senior administrator, or advancement staff member already on board who can take on the task. Whoever you select from within the organization should have prior capital campaign fundraising experience in order to be able to plan effectively.

There are potential downsides to using an internal staff member. These include: lack of available time off from his or her regular job to write a good plan; lack of appropriate experience and depth in campaign work; and the lack

LIVE & LEARN

At a private secondary school, the campaign chair was ready to solicit a parent for $100,000 for their new science building. The parent was relatively unknown to the school's volunteers and had only recently moved into the community.

The school's advancement director had just purchased an electronic prospect-screening program. When he ran the prospect's name through the program, he found that the parent owned over $100 million in stock in a family company that had been bought out by a major conglomerate.

The campaign chair increased the ask amount to $1 million. The parent ultimately made a gift of $3 million to name the new building.

of perspective, or the ability to look at the organization from the outside in. It can be difficult or even politically hazardous for an internal person to make critical comments about organizational or staffing issues that could affect the campaign. These concerns can be remedied if the nonprofit turns to either an outside volunteer or an outside consultant with relevant skills.

A second possibility is to identify a knowledgeable board member or volunteer who can help lead the campaign planning process for your organization. Look for an individual who has prior experience in campaign fundraising and strong analytical skills. A volunteer or board member who is familiar with marketing, strategic planning, or public relations might be a good choice, since these fields are closely tied to fundraising.

Using a volunteer will save your organization both time and money, especially if the individual already is knowledgeable about your mission and goals. Volunteers with relevant professional expertise can bring both an internal and external perspective to bear on your planning issues, which can be very help-ful. A board member or volunteer can also command a level of respect for his or her work that might be lacking if the plan is written internally.

There are, however, some potential pitfalls with using a volunteer. In most business endeavors, you get what you pay for, and even a highly skilled individual who is volunteering her services may not give your campaign plan the time and effort that it deserves. A board member or volunteer may approach issues of orga-nizational staffing and planning with preconceived biases that skew their objec-tivity. It also can be very awkward for the nonprofit if the plan submitted by a volunteer who has donated her time is viewed as flawed or poorly executed.

The third option for preparing a campaign plan is to hire outside counsel. Some organizations hire a consultant just to prepare the campaign plan, while others select a consultant who will work with them during the entire course of the campaign. Campaign consultants have become a fixture of many cam-paigns, and the pros and cons of hiring consultants, as well as what to look for in a consultant, are covered in more detail in the following pages.

Creating the Campaign Plan

Your organization's major stakeholders should participate in the campaign planning process. Hold information sessions, ask for advice, and meet one-on-one with key leaders. Consensus is built through involvement. Ask for input from your board members, volunteers, donors, advancement staff, and the orga-nization's leadership outside of development. You may want to add other con-stituencies, such as lapsed donors, new prospects, and past leaders in order to broaden the insights gained in the planning process.

Most campaign plans contain an analysis of the organization's internal strengths and weaknesses, a review of the external environment for the campaign, and practical and strategic recommendations for conducting the campaign. Some planners include extensive lists of prospects in the campaign plan; others view

EXHIBIT 2.1

Basic Components
of a Capital Campaign Plan

- *Challenges and Opportunities in the External Environment:* Provides a brief overview of economic, social, and philanthropic trends in the region that might affect the campaign.

- *Internal Strengths and Weaknesses of the Organization:* Analyzes the organizational, leadership, and strategic issues of the nonprofit that might affect the outcome of the campaign.

- *Feasibility Study (if one has been conducted):* Identifies the capacity of the known donor pool to meet the projected financial goals of the campaign.

- *Preliminary Campaign Goal:* Recommends a preliminary dollar goal based on fundraising potential, needs, and the feasibility study (if one was done).

- *Timetable and Phasing of the Campaign:* Recommends a set timetable for each phase of the campaign (i.e., the Quiet Phase, the Campaign Kick-off, and the Public Phase).

- *The Case for the Campaign:* Identifies key themes of the case that will be used to encourage donors to support the campaign.

- *Campaign Leadership and Volunteer Structure:* Recommends an organizational structure for campaign volunteers; may list names of potential campaign chairs or co-chairs.

- *Leadership Gift Fundraising:* Identifies strategies and methods for securing the top gifts that will make the campaign succeed.

- *Staffing and Budget:* Recommendations for staffing and budget required for the campaign to succeed.

EXHIBIT 2.1 (CONTINUED)

- *Campaign Gift Table:* Develops several versions of the pyramid-style chart that identifies how many gifts are needed at each dollar level to meet the goal.

- *Major Gift Prospects:* Lists the names and the expected giving level of known prospects deemed capable of making major gifts to the campaign.

---

prospect identification as an early task for staff and volunteers. The standard components of a capital campaign plan are described in Exhibit 2.1.

The campaign plan, or an executive summary, should be presented to staff leaders, the president, the board, relevant committees, and volunteer leaders. It should be revised, if necessary, and formally adopted for approval by the board. Having a written and approved campaign plan allows all the constituents of the nonprofit to reach agreement on the important strategic components of the capital campaign.

Without a plan, you run the risk that the organizational leadership becomes fractured and the organization fails to reach its goal. The mark of a successful campaign is that it becomes the means of uniting all the stakeholders of the organization behind a widely shared and clearly articulated vision and goal. Approving the campaign plan becomes a means of reaching this end.

Campaign Consultants and Feasibility Studies

Do You Need a Campaign Consultant?

Campaign consultants have become an integral part of the campaign planning process. There are many reasons to carefully weigh the pros and cons of bringing in an external consultant to work on your capital campaign. You will need to take into account the level of expertise available on your staff, particularly that of your chief development officer. It can be expensive and time-consuming in the long run to learn how to run a capital campaign while you are in one. The cost to your organization of mistakes and missed opportunities may be more than if you had hired outside expertise to begin with.

Pros (Reasons to Hire a Consultant):

- *Provides objectivity and enhanced credibility.* A consultant is usually able to analyze the organization's strengths and weaknesses without preconceived biases, leading to greater credibility.

- *Brings prior campaign experience.* A consultant brings ideas of what works and what doesn't work from other campaigns so that you don't have to reinvent the wheel.

- *Increases productivity.* A consultant can focus on specific campaign tasks and get them done quickly because of prior experience.

Cons (Reasons Not to Hire a Consultant):

- *Increases expenses.* Hiring a consultant usually costs more than having staff or volunteers do the same work.

- *Applies standardized methodology.* Some consulting firms use a standard cookie-cutter approach that they apply to all campaigns that may not fit your organization's needs.

- *Requires a Learning Curve.* A consultant has to quickly learn your organization's strengths, weaknesses, and how to appeal to your donors.

How to Hire a Consultant

Decide in advance what you want from a consultant. Do you want someone who will write the campaign plan and help conduct a feasibility study? Do you need a full-service consultant who will stay with your organization throughout the campaign? Do you want someone in your area who can work with your staff side by side, or someone who flies in for one day a month? The better you can define your needs in advance, the more success you will have in identifying a consultant who will meet your needs.

Finding good outside counsel can be a challenge. Make sure that you present your campaign and your organization completely and honestly to potential consulting partners, for you will get the best results from someone who understands your organization, warts and all. You want someone who will communicate with you directly and honestly, but who is sensitive to your needs.

TIPS & TECHNIQUES

When Hiring a Campaign Consultant:

- Talk to colleagues in AFP or other peers for names of possible firms.

- Interview more than one firm to compare costs, services, and experience.

- Ask who will work on your account and meet with him in person.

- Use volunteers, board members, and staff to help you select the firm.

- Choose a firm experienced in campaigns similar in size and type to yours.

- Ask for a written contract that spells out the services to be provided.

- Hire a firm for a small project to test its work before signing a contract.

Consultants can be paid by the hour, by the project, or put on a retainer. *AFP considers it unethical to pay consultants a straight percentage of a gift made to the campaign.* This is viewed as poor fundraising practice because it deprives the organization of the full benefit of the gift and it can anger donors who feel their gift should be used to further the mission and purposes of the nonprofit. The practice can also encourage consultants to close a small, short-term gift (from which they can derive immediate benefit) in preference to working on a larger, long-term gift that might take more time to close, thus hurting the organization in the long run.

Campaign Feasibility Studies

A campaign feasibility study is a marketing study designed to help your organization learn more about the reception your campaign might receive from various external audiences. Most studies include market research, often obtained through conducting interviews, that is designed to test certain assumptions about giving or attitudes of potential donors.

The best study results are usually derived from personal, face-to-face interviews with a carefully selected cohort of supporters and leaders of the organization. External consultants often conduct these studies because they have the time and expertise and can provide a fresh perspective. A consultant can often elicit comments from a study participant that the participant might not make to a staff member. A study can be one component of creating the campaign plan, and often campaign consultants will provide a feasibility study as one component of the campaign planning process.

RULES OF THE ROAD

Never date a donor.

There are many reasons for deciding to conduct a campaign feasibility study (see Exhibit 2.2). The most common reason to conduct a campaign feasibility study is to determine whether the preliminary goal can be reached. Conducting a feasibility study is also a good way to cultivate prospective leadership donors, because the purpose of the study is to ask for their advice and input.

It is important to understand, however, that there are limitations to the techniques employed in such studies, since they rely on personal interaction between the prospect and the interviewer. The answers they provide may not be completely reliable, especially when a prospective donor is asked how much he will give to a certain organization.

In most communities, a well-recognized cohort of wealthy philanthropists is surveyed over and over again for these studies, and many of them have

---

EXHIBIT 2.2

Reasons for Conducting a Campaign Feasibility Study

Conduct a Campaign Study:

- To cultivate your top prospects by asking for their advice and involvement

- To determine how committed your donors are to the campaign

- To test the feasibility of your fundraising goal

- To learn where you rank in your prospects' giving priorities

- To see how prospects react to your case statement and themes

- To test your appeal to new potential supporters

- To learn how others perceive your organization and its goals

IN THE REAL WORLD

The Feasibility Study

In one recent capital campaign, a precampaign feasibility study was under-taken by an outside consulting firm. The consultant said the organization could raise about $8 million, but the campaign eventually surpassed $20 million, an amount 2.5 times larger than the study predicted. Why was the study so off base?

In retrospect, many of the prospects interviewed responded very con-servatively when asked how much they would give. Once the campaign began, they were given more time to learn about the organization's needs and goals. The gifts they actually made were substantially higher than the level they had indicated to the consultant at the outset.

In addition, as the campaign progressed, volunteers identified new prospects who eventually made major gifts. Because these prospects had not been part of the feasibility study, the original goal projection didn't include their potential gifts.

become increasingly reluctant to reveal their future giving plans. In today's uncertain economic environment, they may not even know their future giving plans. Therefore, it is prudent to view the results from a feasibility study as one data point among several other considerations in setting the goal.

Campaign Budget and Staffing

How Much Should You Budget for Your Campaign?

Begin by calculating your current fundraising expenditures in terms of cost per dollar raised, which is a useful mechanism for comparison between like insti-tutions. In general, because of the extensive use of volunteers and the focus on

TIPS & TECHNIQUES

Plan for campaign efficiency. *It is less expensive to raise big gifts than smaller ones.* Focus on a smaller number of large gifts to save time and money for your campaign. Smaller donors often require the same amount of attention from staff, volunteers, gift processing, donor services, and stewardship as large donors (and sometimes more!).

large gifts, it costs less (in terms of cost per dollar raised) to fundraise during a campaign than it does to raise annual gifts for ongoing operational support.

Campaign costs vary widely. The cost can be as low as 3 cents on the dollar, and as high as 50 cents on the dollar. A recommended range is from 8 to16 cents per dollar raised. If, for example, you want to raise $10 million over five years (an average of $2 million per year), the campaign budget should be between $160,000 and $320,000 per year (calculated as a range of 8 to16% of $2 million). Note that this is the incremental cost of the campaign, and it should be added to the ongoing budget for advancement, assuming that normal fundraising programs will continue during the campaign period.

In any event, if you want to raise more, you will have to spend more. Even with a lower cost per dollar raised, you will have to spend more total dollars for fundraising than you did before the campaign. The good news is that you will also be raising more money.

Some Issues to Consider When Planning Your Campaign Budget:

- *Will there be one-time costs up front?* Special costs in the first year include: campaign feasibility studies, campaign publications, and heavier use of campaign consultants for training, writing the campaign plan, and organizing the campaign.

- *Who will be making the calls and asking for money?* Assess the strength and skill level of your organization's volunteer base. Many organizations are moving to a more staff-driven fundraising model for their capital campaigns as volunteers become burned out or too busy, but hiring experienced major gifts staff can be very expensive.

- *Where will most of your prospects be located?* It costs more to mount a national campaign than it does to fundraise from local or regional prospects. Added costs for national campaigns include more staff travel, more events, and increased phone and mail costs.

- *Consider outsourcing certain tasks.* Outsourcing can be cost effective in areas with specific objectives, such as publication design, Web site development, event planning, and direct mail.

- *How good is the current development office infrastructure?* During a campaign, the development infrastructure faces increased demands from volunteers, staff, and donors. You may need to invest in areas such as gift processing and information systems to support the enhanced activity level of a capital campaign.

Campaign Staffing Functions

There are a variety of development functions that will have to be covered during a capital campaign (see Exhibit 2.3). Analyze both your current development staff capacity and your campaign needs to determine whether you should hire new staff, bundle some functions together, add functions to current staff members' job descriptions, hire consultants, or identify outside contractors. There is no one-size-fits-all staffing plan; some small organizations contract out all campaign activities, while larger organizations may double the size of their staff during a campaign.

Don't automatically assume that your current staff can't take on additional responsibilities, even if they are very busy with current assignments. Many development staff members welcome a campaign as a time to learn new skills, move up the career ladder, and showcase hidden talents. Providing opportunities to current staff can build confidence, improve skills, and inspire personal and professional growth. Improving training and cross training can help current and new staff update skills and build a team attitude.

EXHIBIT 2.3

Campaign Staffing and Functions

Note: How many staff will be needed for each function depends on the size and complexity of your campaign.

Staff	Function
Campaign Director	Directs and manages campaign activity
Major Gifts	Cultivates and asks individuals for larger gifts
Corporate Giving	Cultivates and asks corporations for campaign gifts
Foundation Giving	Cultivates and asks foundations for campaign gifts
Planned Giving	Markets planned giving program to campaign donors
Volunteer Coordinator	Oversees and directs campaign volunteer activity
Prospect Researcher	Provides research on campaign prospects
Proposal Writer	Prepares proposals for campaign prospects
Donor Stewardship	Recognition and reporting on gift activity to donor
Event Planning	Plans and manages all campaign events
Public Relations	Provides PR and media support for campaign
Direct Mail Coordinator	Supervises direct mail component of campaign

---

EXHIBIT 2.3 (CONTINUED)

Publications Director	Writes and designs campaign brochures, newsletters
Web Site Designer	Provides Web content, design, and management
Data Entry	Records addresses, contact, and tracking information
Gift Processing	Processes campaign gifts and acknowledgments
Pledge Reminder	Manages system for mailing reminders to donors
Information Systems	Manages data, lists, and produces reports
Administrative Support	Provides reception, typing, filing, phone, and so on

---

Paying for the Campaign

There are no magic tricks when it comes to paying for a capital campaign. Many nonprofits capitalize the total campaign costs in their budget and raise the campaign goal to offset the costs on a long-term basis. Some campaigns run two separate budgets for the advancement area during a capital campaign: one for ongoing operational fundraising that will continue after the campaign is completed, and one for specific expenses that are tied to the capital campaign.

Some Options to Review When Considering How to Pay for Your Capital Campaign:

- Defer campaign costs, increase the goal by the amount of the costs, and pay them out of the campaign fundraising results.

- Defer campaign costs and pay them out of increased operating income after the campaign is completed.

- Take out a loan and repay it out of future gifts or operations.

- Raise special gifts or grants that can be used to cover campaign costs.

- Devote a portion of endowment income for a period of years to cover campaign costs.

- Use unrestricted bequests and one-time gifts to pay for the campaign.

- Hold a special event or fundraiser to pay for campaign costs.

TIPS & TECHNIQUES

Ideas for Reducing Campaign Costs:

- Ask volunteers to help with event planning, publications, and PR.

- Double up on functions: have your annual fund person make lower-level campaign solicitations; ask your proposal writer to draft campaign brochures.

- Hire lower-level staff who cost less initially, then provide more training.

- Use desktop publishing tools for printed materials.

- Use less expensive materials, like preprinted folders and paper.

- Hold a contest to pick your campaign name and logo.

- Cut travel costs by utilizing more e-mail and phone contact.

- Create inexpensive PowerPoint presentations for calls on prospects.

- Plan events in volunteers' homes or corporate facilities provided for free.

Be sure to get board approval for whatever method you choose. Sometimes donors will ask how these costs are being managed, and your answer could affect your ability to receive a gift from them.

Summary

A campaign plan brings together all the constituents of the organization to create a blueprint for a united effort. Many organizations find it useful to hire a consultant and conduct a campaign feasibility study to aid them in their planning process. Staffing and budget needs also must be addressed as part of the preparation for campaign activity. The campaign planning process offers a unique opportunity to involve the organization's stakeholders in helping to set future directions and goals.

CHAPTER 3

Campaign Structure: Timetables, Gift Tables, and Goals

After reading this chapter, you will be able to:

- Plan the timetable for your campaign.
- Develop and use a campaign gift table.
- Set a realistic campaign goal.

Choosing the Right Timetable

Timing is an important element of campaign strategy. Most capital campaigns are multiyear efforts, and many campaigns are divided into two or more phases. Each phase is marked by interim goals and the solicitation of targeted constituencies. The time frame of each phase must be long enough to achieve the desired goal, but short enough so that staff, volunteers, and campaign leaders stay focused on the tasks at hand.

Selecting the right timetable for your campaign can help to build momentum, an elusive but critical component of all successful fundraising efforts. A campaign achieves momentum when a number of gifts at significant levels begin to come in, creating a growing sense among the organization's supporters that the campaign can't help but succeed. When your prospects feel that they need to give now, or they will be left out, and you sense an increasing swell of support, then you have created momentum for your campaign. This sense of building toward the inevitable, yet successful, conclusion of the campaign is partly the result of choosing the right timetable for your organization.

The Quiet Phase

In the traditional two-phase campaign, the first phase is called the nucleus fund, the leadership gift phase, or the quiet phase. It is a highly focused, well-defined drive to bring in substantial early support for the campaign, usually in the form of leadership or major gifts. The quiet phase is designed to solicit gifts from those donors who are already close to the organization and who can be counted on to lead the way for others who might need more time or more cultivation before they will commit to the cause.

Some organizations also use the quiet phase to test a preliminary goal before publicly announcing the campaign goal. Another advantage of having a quiet phase is that you can make small adjustments in your campaign marketing components, like elements of the case. The quiet phase is also the time to finalize architectural plans and costs if you are constructing a building.

The board leadership, the campaign chairs, and the campaign committee members should be solicited during the quiet phase. The quiet phase usually relies on peer-to-peer personal solicitations for high-level gifts. Who solicits whom depends on the nonprofit's sense of protocol and organizational hierarchy, as well as practical factors such as whether a campaign chair has been recruited as the campaign's quiet phase opens.

In some organizations, the executive director or president solicits the board chair, who then in turn solicits the campaign leadership and other members of

TIPS & TECHNIQUES

Board Solicitation Guidelines during the Quiet Phase:

- In many campaigns, giving from members of the board accounts for as much as one-third to one-half of the total goal.

- The campaign chair or the consultant should talk to the entire board about their giving responsibilities at the beginning of the campaign.

- As a rule, like any campaign volunteer, a board member should have made her own gift before soliciting others.

- Both the campaign chair and the board chair should be asked for a gift very early in the quiet phase.

- The executive director can play a key role in the solicitation of board members, but a peer should also be included in the meetings.

the board. In other cases, the campaign chair begins the process by soliciting the board chair and campaign committee members. Once they have made their own commitments, the campaign committee members then solicit the remaining board members. The goal is to get the maximum possible participation, coupled with a strong financial showing, so that going forward into the campaign the volunteers can point to substantial support from the board and campaign leadership.

Early high-level gifts are particularly important to close during this phase. The size of the gifts during the quiet phase usually sets the range for the size of most of the gifts that you will receive during the rest of the campaign. While this might not seem logical, because large gifts can be closed at any point during a campaign, once a number of gifts have been made and the quiet phase is closing, it is difficult to push the dollar level of gifts up past the range of giving that was established during this early period.

In some campaigns there develops an informal "cluster" approach to campaign giving by board members and other leaders in the group. Based on early gifts from peers, it becomes understood that a certain level of gift (say $25,000) is appropriate from members of the "inner circle," more or less regardless of capacity. This results in a situation where no one in the group gives much more (and few give less). The strategy to deal with this, from an organizational viewpoint, is to carefully plan ahead and seed the early phase of the campaign with gifts of the level you will need for success.

Some organizations also solicit internal constituencies, such as staff or faculty, at this point to demonstrate internal support for the campaign. The quiet phase can take months or years, but it should be short enough to create momentum and long enough to set a strong pace for giving in the remainder of the campaign.

Most campaigns set a percentage of the total campaign goal as their benchmark for the quiet phase of the campaign. Many campaigns today reach 50 to 70% of their goal during this early phase. The strategy behind this push is that it allows them to have a higher proportion of the campaign dollars in hand when the campaign goes public. Having such a large percentage of the funds in hand gives the public phase of the campaign a boost, and it shows the level of commitment from the board and the campaign leadership. All this is calculated to give potential donors the assurance that the campaign will succeed.

The Public Phase

The public phase of the campaign has two objectives: meeting the campaign goal and expanding the campaign to reach broader constituencies. This phase, as its name suggests, requires more marketing and outreach to bring the campaign to a wider audience. In the public phase, fundraisers look for gifts from

IN THE REAL WORLD

Raising Sights for Donors at All Giving Levels

An art museum completed its first capital campaign by recognizing all donors of $5,000 and up on a beautiful, permanent bronze plaque mounted in their lobby. As they planned their next capital campaign, several years later, the advancement team decided to mount a new plaque in the new wing, but they raised the entry-level gift for recognition to $25,000.

The strategy was very effective, and allowed them to go back to donors to their earlier campaign and solicit gifts of $25,000 from donors who had previously given them $5,000 or $10,000. Their donors wanted to be on the wall, and raising the entry-level gift for recognition didn't discourage them.

lower-level donors and reach out to new donor groups, while continuing to cultivate and close higher-level gifts from prospects who may require additional cultivation or more time before making a commitment.

A wide variety of fundraising tools can come into play in the public phase. Campaigns commonly make use of tools that provide for broader outreach at this stage, including direct mail, telemarketing, newspaper and radio ads, Internet marketing, and community-wide brick campaigns. Volunteer outreach is an important component of all phases of a campaign, but volunteers might be used in a different manner during each phase (see Exhibit 3.1).

Alternative Timetables

Not all campaigns have just a quiet phase and a public phase. The timetable you select depends on your organization's unique circumstances and needs.

45

Five Alternative Timetables to Consider:

- *Phase by timing of construction.* Raise money for different components of a building, or for more than one building, on a sequential basis. Coordinate the construction schedule and the fundraising schedule.

- *Phase by geographic region.* Announce the campaign in different parts of the country at different times. Start locally, and then open the campaign in targeted cities on a rolling basis.

- *Phase by different gift types.* Solicit cash and pledges early in the campaign, and then follow up with a planned giving push to build future gifts for endowment and program support.

- *Phase by the type of funding needed.* Develop separate phases for capital, operational, and endowment needs. Combine them in one total but fundraise for each on a separate timetable.

- *Phase by constituency or organizational units.* In a complex organization, such as a university, plan to have one unit (such as the medical center) fundraise in the first phase, and then follow with other units.

EXHIBIT 3.1

Sample Timetable for a Three-Year, $10 Million Capital Campaign

Preparing for the Campaign

- Create a campaign plan and hire a campaign consultant if desired.
- Prepare Table of Needs, complete architectural plans, get costs.
- Confirm board support of the project and the campaign plan.

Year 1: Begin Leadership Gift Phase (raise $4 million)

- Recruit campaign co-chairs and campaign committee members.

EXHIBIT 3.1 (CONTINUED)

- Solicit leadership gifts from board, co-chairs, and campaign committee.

- Focus on prospects of $100,000+, assign them to volunteers.

Year 2: Begin Public Phase (raise additional $3 million)

- Hold campaign kick-off event to begin public phase.

- Plan small group events to cultivate new prospects.

- Solicit major gifts of $25,000 to $100,000.

Year 3: Complete the Public Phase (reach the $10 million goal)

- Broaden base of lower-level support through direct mail and telemarketing.

- Focus on donations of $1,000 to $25,000.

- Finish solicitation of all prospects at all levels.

At the Finish Line: Closing the Campaign

- Hold an event to end the campaign, such as a building dedication.

- Thank and honor campaign leaders, volunteers, and donors.

- Provide donor stewardship through building signage and recognition.

Gift Tables

Using Gift Tables in Campaign Planning

If fundraising is both an art and a science, then gift tables are the point at which the two converge. Gift tables are a calculated effort to mathematically determine the number of gifts and donors that will be required at different dollar levels to reach the campaign goal. Attempting to predict the number and level of gifts that might appear during a campaign is a little like handicapping a political race; you know what the polls say, you can guess who is out ahead, but you really don't know where things stand until it's all over.

Gift tables are also known as gift or donor pyramids, because, when illustrated, they usually form a pyramid, or sloping, shape. The basic model shows a small number of donors making gifts at the top, a moderate number of donors making gifts at the middle levels, and a large number of donors making gifts at the bottom levels. Campaign planners find that this model of graduated gifts holds true for campaigns of almost every size and type.

Gift tables are used as a planning tool in many ways. Their primary purpose is to help determine how many prospects are needed at different levels of the giving pyramid to reach the required dollar totals. They can be useful in guiding the planning of pricing of various recognition opportunities. Some

TIPS & TECHNIQUES

Uses for Gift Tables:

- To determine if there are enough prospects identified at each gift level to make the campaign goal reachable

- To assist in defining the campaign structure and financial goals

- To price naming opportunities and recognition for donors at various levels

- To raise sights among board members and campaign leaders

- To serve as a visual aid on solicitation calls with prospects solicitors like to bring them along on calls to help illustrate potential gift levels and the number of gifts needed in front of prospective donors.

Making a Gift Table That Fits Your Organization

- *Assume that you will need three or four prospects for each gift.* This ratio depends on how close you are to your donors and how well you have cultivated them in advance of the capital campaign.

- *Identify the highest-level gift that will be made to the campaign.* The top-level gift is usually at least 10% of the campaign total, and can be as much as 30 to 50% of the total, depending on the size of the campaign and the project being undertaken. Also consider the giving capacity of the prospects available.

- *Identify lower levels of giving based on standard gift ranges such as $500,000, $250,000, $100,000, and $50,000.* The number of gifts needed at each level should be about twice the number of gifts needed at the next level above. Work across the chart, multiplying the number of gifts needed by the dollar amount to arrive at the total dollars raised for each gift level.

- *Identify attractive recognition opportunities to match each gift level.* Naming the outside of the building is a popular way to recognize the largest gift in the campaign, while naming of internal spaces may be offered to donors of lower-level gifts.

- *Fill in each gift level with known prospects based on their capacity to give.* The goal is to fill out each level of the gift table with identified prospects who can be cultivated and solicited for your campaign.

Sample Gift Tables

Gift tables illustrate an important campaign rule: that raising a few more gifts at the top levels can relieve you from the effort of raising hundreds more gifts at the lower levels.

The level of the highest gift is the most important element in developing the gift table for your campaign. The difference between planning for a top gift of $500,000 and a top gift of $1,000,000 can be dramatic in a campaign with a goal of $3,000,000 (see Exhibit 3.2).

Note that the number of gifts needed at the bottom half of the table drops quickly for the campaign with the higher lead gift (Exhibit 3.2, sample II). This campaign will require less work for the staff and volunteers, less money spent on reaching lower-level donors, and less time to reach the goal.

EXHIBIT 3.2

Two Sample Gift Tables for a $3,000,000 Capital Campaign

Sample I: Top Gift at $500,000

Gift Level	Prospects	Donors	Dollars	% of Campaign
$ 500,000	3	1	$ 500,000	17%
$ 250,000	6	2	$ 500,000	17%
$ 100,000	12	4	$ 400,000	13%
$ 50,000	24	8	$ 400,000	13%
$ 25,000	48	16	$ 400,000	13%
$ 10,000	96	32	$ 320,000	11%
$ 5,000	192	64	$ 320,000	11%
$ 1,000 and below	numerous		$ 160,000	5%
Total Raised			**$ 3,000,000**	

EXHIBIT 3.2 (CONTINUED)

Sample II: Top Gift at $1,000,000

Gift Level	Prospects	Donors	Dollars	% of Campaign
$1,000,000	3	1	$1,000,000	33%
$ 500,000	3	1	$ 500,000	17%
$ 250,000	6	2	$ 500,000	17%
$ 100,000	9	3	$ 300,000	10%
$ 50,000	18	6	$ 300,000	10%
$ 25,000	24	8	$ 200,000	6.5%
$ 10,000	60	20	$ 200,000	6.5%
Total Raised			**$ 3,000,000**	

Setting the Goal

Setting Realistic Goals

Setting the goal for your campaign may be a simple or a complex process, depending on your organization's needs and level of sophistication. You should analyze your organization's needs, its past giving patterns, and its future gift potential to determine the goal that best fits your capability. Peer campaign fundraising levels can also be a useful benchmark.

Ideally, a goal should stretch the organization's fundraising capability but still be realistic within the time frame of the campaign. If the goal is too high, you will struggle to reach it and possibly fail, which could hurt the organization, disappoint donors, and blunt future support. If the goal is too low, you could miss out on an opportunity to realize gifts that might help your organization for years to come.

Techniques for Goal Setting

There is more than one method for determining what your goal should be. The two main considerations in setting campaign goals are: how much you need and how much you can raise.

The techniques described here can help you put numbers to these concerns. You may want to use all these methods and see where they converge. In the final analysis, though, the board, the executive director, and the chief advancement officer should all approve the final goal. It is not productive to have a key leader, whether volunteer or staff, who doesn't support the goal. If this situation arises, either bring in a consultant to do a feasibility study, or set a preliminary goal within a range to help resolve the situation.

Techniques for Setting Realistic Goals:

- *Put a price to your needs.* Many organizations conduct a strategic planning exercise to determine their needs before starting a campaign (see Chapter 1). These needs should then be prioritized, with costs estimated for each need. For a bricks-and-mortar campaign, hire an architect and get an estimate of the construction costs. Be sure to consider the full costs—including enhancements in program, endowment, maintenance, operations, staffing, and construction—that will be required to build, open, and run a new program or facility.

 RULES OF THE ROAD

Don't count on a gift until it's in writing (e-mail doesn't count).

- *Analyze past giving.* Become familiar with your organization's past giving patterns. Even with the enhanced activity of a campaign, these patterns will probably not change radically. To be realistic, project future giving levels during each campaign year in reasonable increments over what your organization has raised, as an average, each year for the past five years.

  For instance, if your organization averages $100,000 per year in total fundraising, then you may be able to raise 50% more ($150,000), or twice as much ($200,000), but probably not five times more ($500,000). A campaign goal that requires you to raise more than twice the amount of past giving may be unrealistic, unless there are unusual circumstances at work.

- *Evaluate and rate your potential donors.* Rate the giving potential of your prospect list, including board members and current and previous donors. For new prospects, add only those whom you realistically think you can reach during the campaign period. Rate each of them for the maximum gift you think they could give if they were properly cultivated and solicited.

  Place the prospects in their appropriate slot on your gift table and see if you have enough names at each level. (Using campaign leaders or members of your board to help rate prospects for this exercise can be very instructive, and often helps those leaders think about their own gifts.) If you have large gaps in your gift table, you will need to either adjust your goal or find some new ways to identify more prospects for your campaign.

- *Conduct a feasibility study.* While feasibility studies are not always completely accurate at predicting campaign results, they do represent a useful data point in the goal-setting process (see Chapter 2). If you hire a consultant to conduct a study, you can also use the study to help cultivate prospective donors and determine where your organization stands in their philanthropic priorities.

LIVE & LEARN

A capital campaign for a new wing at the city's art museum set a goal of $75 million. The board included several entrepreneurs who had started successful companies and were worth hundreds of millions. One of them was selected chair of the campaign, and he started soliciting his fellow board members.

A competitive spirit quickly developed among the more entrepreneurial board members, and several challenged each other to make large gifts to "set the pace" for the campaign. The chair made his own gift of $10 million, and the others responded in kind. In 18 months the campaign goal was met without one single solicitation outside the board ever having been made. The campaign never even moved into its public phase.

- *Look to your peers.* Study how much your peer institutions have raised in their most recent capital campaigns. Analyze any relevant factors that might make your organization more or less effective than these peers in fundraising. These factors might include differences in your region, your size, special constituencies, or past giving patterns. Make an assessment of whether you could match or surpass their capital campaign goals.

Adjusting Goals for Changing Circumstances

The economic environment must be factored into your campaign goal planning. Most donors, whatever their source of wealth may be, are dependent on economic growth to produce the income that supports their philanthropic gifts. If the economy falters, as measured by the stock market, employment, or

TIPS & TECHNIQUES

Often the goal may need adjustment up or down as your campaign progresses. Here are several methods to build this flexibility into your campaign plan.

Options for Adjusting the Campaign Goal:

- *Use the quiet phase as a test for the final goal.* Set a preliminary target; for example, 50% of the total goal will be raised from leadership gifts. If early gifts are low, then lower your public goal.

- *Set the goal as a range, rather than choosing one number.* Set an initial goal ranging, say, between $40 million and $50 million. After the quiet phase, when your lead gifts are in hand, decide which number you will use.

- *Design the campaign in sequential phases.* Plan a second phase of the facility that could be built out after the initial construction is completed, or build your facility one section at a time.

- *Stretch out your timetable.* Add extra time for more fundraising. Raising $15 million over three years (average annual goal: $5 million) is harder than raising $15 million over five years (average annual goal: $3 million).

- *Cut back on project costs.* This may be necessary if fundraising falls short. "Value engineering" is the term used for cutting costs in construction by using less expensive materials and cutting back on extras.

- *Extend the campaign and raise the goal.* Implement this strategy toward the end of a campaign if you still have untapped potential prospects. Use it to keep a successful effort going, or to add new needs, such as endowment.

corporate earnings, your donors' ability to make gifts or to pay on pledges already made could change abruptly.

The growth of philanthropic activity in the United States has historically correlated very closely with the growth of the stock market. Not surprisingly, then, if the market declines, giving will decline, no matter how attractive and urgent a campaign might appear. In the past few years, national giving trends have shown that even the fear of losing assets can affect philanthropic activity.

As the threats of war and international terrorism have affected the stability of our economy, some segments of our philanthropic sector have cut back on their giving, at least temporarily. Some individuals and many of the largest foundations have lost considerable assets in the stock market, which has affected their capacity to give. You must assess the chances for the success of your campaign in the political and financial environment in which you are operating. Read *The Wall Street Journal*, subscribe to your local business journal, and keep an eye on the stock market to see trends that could affect your donors.

Goal setting has some important psychological ramifications. It can be dangerous to set a goal too high, and fail to reach it; but on the other hand, many experienced fundraisers set a "stretch goal" as a way to stimulate larger gifts and energize the donor base. Some nonprofits have a higher capacity for taking risks than others. Sometimes presidents want to attract attention to their leadership, and for them, a big vision can be signaled by a big goal. Each organization must look at all the issues involved and come to a determination of what is the best, most reasonable, most achievable goal for its own needs.

Summary

The decisions you make about your campaign's structure and goals are important components of the overall campaign strategy. In many campaigns, the timetable includes two phases: the quiet phase, in which the focus is on soliciting the leadership and those prospects at the top of the gift table, and the

A hospital was preparing to kick off a capital campaign with a goal of $100 million. The CEO and the board chairperson wanted to put on a gala kick-off event that would really wow all their prospective donors. The event was so complex that it required the full attention of every member of the advancement staff for six months before the event. Even though over $1 million total was raised from the event, the hospital netted only $350,000 for six months' work due to the huge costs of the event.

After the event was over, the advancement staff focused their efforts on major gift fundraising with their campaign chair. In only three weeks of intense fundraising activity, the chair raised over $5 million from three leadership donors. They all learned that major gift fundraising brings in more money given the time and effort spent than large events do.

public phase, in which gifts are solicited from a broad base of lower-level donors. How much you raise from your board and campaign leaders, and the size of the earliest gifts, can influence giving levels throughout the campaign.

Gift tables are a planning tool that helps to predict the number of gifts needed at each gift level to reach the campaign goal. Setting a reasonable goal requires taking into account a variety of factors, from the needs of your organization to the giving potential of your top prospects. Finally, preliminary goals can be adjusted in a number of ways as the campaign takes shape and gifts begin to come in.

CHAPTER 4

Effective Campaign Leadership

After reading this chapter, you will be able to:

- Enhance board leadership of your campaign.
- Set an appropriate role for your president and staff.
- Create a volunteer structure and manage volunteers successfully.

Board Leadership in the Capital Campaign

Nonprofit organizations are only as good as their boards. Board leadership is a more critical factor to the success of capital campaigns than in the course of any other activity the organization pursues. The board must be able to provide energy, leadership, passion, commitment, and time to make the campaign work. It is also preferable if the board can provide a substantial portion of the campaign dollars needed, but where this isn't possible, alternatives can be devised. While it is also preferable if the board includes skilled fundraisers, training, good planning, and professional staff, support can work wonders with an able and willing board.

Why the Board Has to Provide Leadership

There are many reasons why boards become the focus of leadership in a capital campaign. The amount of actual fundraising done by board members will vary from organization to organization and from campaign to campaign. In general, advancement staff members and executive directors of nonprofits have been increasingly involved in the planning, direction, and implementation of capital campaigns. However, an effective board is still a requirement for success.

Many organizations wisely undergo a board self-review process a year or two before attempting a major capital fundraising project (see Exhibit 4.1). The size of the board can be expanded; the composition of the board can be altered

TIPS & TECHNIQUES

Roles for Board Members in a Campaign:

- Board members set the pace for leadership gifts by the level of their own giving to the organization.

- Board members are often the peers of other donors in the community and can influence their peers through their own gifts and involvement.

- Board members can be outstanding spokespersons for the organization.

- Board members can open doors to prospects more effectively than staff.

- Boards have a fiduciary responsibility to make the campaign fit into the organization's mission, needs, and financial resources.

- Board members can help build the case by sharing their own responses to the campaign and reasons for giving.

EXHIBIT 4.1

Board Activities to Undertake before a Capital Campaign

- Evaluate and strengthen your board's governance processes.

- Determine if your board is the right size and diversity (racial, demographic, geographic) to represent your mission.

- Recruit new board members *before the campaign begins* who could be donors or help in future fundraising efforts.

- Create an orientation and training program for new board members.

- Identify ways of educating your board members to become knowledgeable, enthusiastic proponents of your mission and services.

- Identify future leaders and create opportunities for them in leadership roles.

or broadened, with new members who bring special expertise in fundraising or access to funding sources brought in early in the process. It is always better to tell new board members your plans when you are recruiting them, even if you haven't publicly announced a campaign. They will be more willing to help if they know where your organization is headed.

How to Help the Board Lead

In a capital campaign, the members of the board apply their leadership role first by their involvement in, and approval of, the capital campaign needs and goals. All capital campaigns should go through a formal approval process where the board assesses the needs, approves the plans, and agrees on the financial goals and timetable. Often this approval process begins at the committee level, but it should ultimately move to the full board for approval.

The board needs to buy in to make a campaign successful, and the buy in starts with a detailed understanding and commitment to the needs and goals of the capital campaign. It is incumbent on staff, consultants, or in some cases, the relevant board committees to explain thoroughly and honestly what is needed, what the financial implications are, and what the long-term effect will be on the organization's ability to meet its mission.

This education process is a key step in building leadership and commitment for the capital campaign among board members. In some cases, it may be obvious to all concerned that a new building has to be built; the old one is crumbling on their heads during meetings. In many organizations, however, a

LIVE & LEARN

A new six-story building was being dedicated on the college campus at the end of a major capital campaign. All the donors and the board had been invited for a gala event that would officially open the new building. As the event began, 15 major donors crowded into the elevator to go up to the sixth floor reception room. The overburdened elevator froze between floors, the lights and air conditioning failed, and the donors stood in the hot, dark, crowded space for over an hour while the repairman was located and brought to the site.

The dedication went on, but a few weeks later the advancement director received a letter from one of the donors. It included the bill from her psychiatrist for the therapy required for her to recover from the elevator experience. The college paid the bill with no comment.

more sophisticated approach to planning should be undertaken. This might include a strategic planning exercise, the hiring of an architect to create a plan, and undertaking the financial planning necessary to demonstrate future growth and needs.

The ultimate point of planning at both the organizational and board level is to both educate and motivate the board so that they will make their own gift and make your organization's case effectively with others. Creating advocates for the campaign on the board requires a climate of open communication, trust, information sharing, and mutual respect between board and staff. If these qualities are lacking (on either side) the capital campaign will suffer.

Techniques for Increased Board Giving

All board members are not created equal in terms of financial capability. While some members may be selected because of their personal wealth or philanthropic interests, there are many other desirable qualities to look for in new members, such as: area of professional expertise, commitment to the mission, experience with and/or access to a sector of the community, government or public service background, personal qualities, and so forth. It has also become increasingly important for fundraising purposes to create a board that is diverse in terms of age, sex, race, and geographic reach.

All board members should be asked to financially support the capital campaign at the beginning of the campaign. This is not only important for meeting the organization's financial goals; it is increasingly important for convincing other prospective donors to give. Many individuals and foundations now routinely ask how much a board has given, or what percentage of the board has given, when they are approached for a gift.

What happens when board members are asked to make gifts to the capital campaign? Some are more able than others. Some are more willing than others. Some will wait to see what the leaders do. Some will look for other, nonmonetary ways to give. There are a few techniques that can assist the organization in working with the board to maximize their commitment to the campaign, both in terms of the money raised and the work provided.

How much should the board give? The answer varies based on the board membership. Some grassroots community organizations may target 100% board giving as their goal; $25 a month for several months may be a generous level for some participants, and they should be made to feel comfortable with what-

TIPS & TECHNIQUES

Goal: to encourage board members to give to their capacity and be willing to share their passion about the organization with others who can give.

How to Increase Board Giving:

- Make sure the board has been adequately educated on the reasons for the capital campaign.

- Identify a few respected leaders on the board and ask them to make the first gifts.

- Ask these first donors to set the pace by making gifts that others will view as a stretch in terms of their capacity.

- Create excitement about the project with architectural renderings, models, videos, marketing materials, and presentations.

- Develop a list of gift levels and naming opportunities that show gifts at a variety of levels and present it to the board.

- Encourage board members who have made early commitments to solicit members who haven't given yet.

- Set a board goal or challenge the board to reach a certain level.

- Recognize gifts and thank donors promptly, publicly (get their permission first!), and often.

ever their situation allows them to give. The case to be made here is that many donors and foundations will want to see participation, rather than dollars, as an indicator of the board's commitment to the campaign.

Many nationally prominent institutions, such as universities and national museums, bring in an average of 30 to 50% of the campaign total in gifts from their boards. Private schools, museums, and cultural organizations can be even higher; one prominent museum recently ran a capital campaign where the goal was met without a single gift from outside the board.

Raising such a high percentage of the goal from the board is the exception and not the rule, however, and may not even be desirable, since one of the important results of the campaign is that it broadens the outreach of the organization by bringing in new donors and supporters.

In order to plan the solicitation of the board, the executive director, board chair, campaign chair, and chief development officer should meet to review board capacity, develop individualized solicitation plans, and monitor board giving. Most board members should be solicited by other board members, preferably using solicitors who have already made their own commitment.

A consultant can be useful in working with the board leadership at this point to provide additional perspective, raise sights, and set appropriate goals. Some boards, for instance, may respond well to a challenge gift from one of their own. Or the board leaders might agree to work to reach a specific goal by a targeted date. The campaign chair, if he is also a board member, can be a strong proponent of board giving at board meetings and in individual solicitations. The goal is to find the best way for the board to weigh in early and weigh in strongly in capital campaign giving.

Role of the President and Advancement Staff

While the role of the board is critical in providing leadership, gifts, access to prospects, and support for the mission, successful campaigns require a heavy

The major benefactor of a community nonprofit passed away. His substantial estate passed to his widow, a lovely woman who had married him after her first husband died. The chairman of the board visited the widow some months after her second husband died, suggesting that perhaps their new building could be named in her husband's honor with a substantial gift.

The woman seemed amenable and agreed to a gift of $2 million, but with one change in the plan: she wanted the building named for her first husband, not the second one (who had left her with all the money). The chairman, of course, agreed.

commitment in time, energy, and passion from the executive director or president and the chief advancement officer. Many campaigns founder because one of these two is either not prepared for, or not committed enough to, the success of the effort. And it is a huge effort—notwithstanding large numbers of volunteers, staff, and consultants, running a capital campaign is a tremendous undertaking.

Articulating the Vision

The key role for the nonprofit CEO in the campaign is to set out the vision for the organization (see Exhibit 4.2). She must also be able to share her vision and passion for the cause with prospective donors, and to communicate how the donor's investment in the capital campaign will move that vision forward.

Many organizations today look for a president who is a proven fundraiser. There is no question that a number of able nonprofit CEOs now cultivate, solicit, and ask for major gifts for their organizations and are productive doing so. Often, they are the leaders who can best and most effectively communicate their excitement and knowledge about the organization to a prospective donor.

It is not always necessary, however, for the CEO to ask for or to close a gift. In many organizations, as long as a development professional or fundraising consultant is allowed to play a role in the prospect meetings, the professional can make the ask, close the gift, and handle follow-up with the donor.

Using Staff Effectively

Many nonprofit organizations are moving to a staff-driven development function, as opposed to the earlier model of a volunteer-driven development function, in implementing their capital campaign fundraising program.

EXHIBIT 4.2

Role of the President or Executive Director in the Capital Campaign

- Define the vision for the organization's future.

- Oversee the planning process for the needs that underlie the campaign.

- Help build the case for why a donor should invest in the organization.

- Engage the board in all aspects of the campaign.

- Staff and budget the campaign as needed.

- Serve as chief spokesperson for the organization and its needs.

- Participate in the cultivation and solicitation of prospective donors.

- Take part in providing good stewardship and recognition for donors.

The norm in most capital campaigns today is for advancement staff to plan, direct, and implement all the aspects of the capital campaign (see Exhibit 4.3 for the role of the chief advancement officer). The model of relying on volunteers and board members to do all the campaign strategy, cultivation, and solicitation has become rarer as campaigns have become more complex. Most volunteers simply don't have the expertise, time, or focus needed to make the substantial commitment that it takes to keep a large capital campaign running smoothly.

Perhaps nowhere has the role of advancement staff changed more than in the use of trained development professionals to ask for and close gifts. Nonprofit leaders have found that experience and training do matter in the process of cultivation and solicitation of major gifts. While many campaigns

EXHIBIT 4.3

Role of the Chief Advancement Officer in the Campaign

- Oversee and participate in the preparation of the campaign plan.

- Manage, support, and implement all campaign activity.

- Oversee development of campaign materials and PR activity.

- Accompany volunteers, board members, and the president on calls.

- Cultivate prospects, ask for money, and close gifts.

- Conduct the "money talk" with prospects (see accompanying text).

- Plan and execute campaign events.

- Oversee management of a system to track prospects and activity.

- Provide timely and accurate reports on progress and activity.

- Provide stewardship and recognition for donors.

still prefer to employ volunteers and peers in their prospect cultivation and solicitation activity, the number of gifts asked for and closed by professional fundraisers on their own is on the rise.

The best method for managing the solicitation process may be to integrate the use of professional staff and volunteers. There are several strategies that combine the use of a professional development officer in prospect cultivation and solicitation while still including a volunteer or peer. The strategy used most often is to have both present as members of the team during the solicitation meeting with the prospect. The volunteer can present the case of the campaign and its needs; then the professional development staffer makes the ask and closes the gift.

Another strategy that involves both staff and volunteers in the solicitation process is referred to as the "money talk." With the money talk, an advancement staff member talks with a prospect about his gift informally in order to help pave the way for a solicitation call from a high-level volunteer or board member. The technique works best when the staff member has a good relationship with the prospect, and the prospect is already cultivated and familiar with the organization's case.

The goals of the meeting are for the staff member to identify the donor's giving interests, sound him out on his readiness for a solicitation, and to begin the conversation about the size and nature of the gift. No actual ask is made; however, in many cases, the donor will specify how he wants to be asked and what he wants to be asked for when given the opportunity to do so.

The concept behind this strategy is that a prospective donor has the opportunity to "try out" the size of his gift, and have his questions answered, in a safe

RULES OF THE ROAD

Cash is always better.

setting where no commitment needs to be made. The meeting also spares the time and embarrassment of high-level volunteers if the prospect is not ready for a commitment, or has substantial concerns about the project that need to be addressed before a successful solicitation can be made.

Following the money talk, the development staffer can brief the CEO or volunteer on the prospect's preferences. This type of previewing of the campaign solicitation helps both the donor and the volunteers feel good about their respective roles, and it uses the staff in an effective manner to help bring about a successful solicitation meeting.

The growing emphasis on staff-driven campaign by no means implies that there is no role for volunteers, the CEO, and board members to play in the capital campaign. To the contrary, the involvement of these players is more important than ever. It simply documents the trend among nonprofits that, given the complexity, size, and sheer length of many ongoing capital campaigns, a professional staff is better equipped and trained to focus on making solicitations, keeping the momentum going, and supporting and tracking prospect activity.

Teamwork and Communication

The campaign, like its namesake in war or the political arena, requires the integration of a broad variety of activities and people to be successful. The leader of the campaign must be able to recruit, train, and motivate an army of supporters, from volunteers to paid staff, and to focus and manage their efforts in a productive manner. Without effective management, campaigns can deteriorate into chaos, disarray, and nonproductive behavior. Examples of campaigns out of control include volunteers who approach prospects without adequate planning or preparation, and staff who become demoralized and cynical about the organization and its goals.

In a nonprofit with a professional development staff, the chief advancement officer is the best person to rally the troops and serve as the team leader.

In smaller organizations, the leadership role may fall to the executive director or to an outside volunteer chair. Some campaigns hire a campaign director to direct the activity; some hire an outside consultant to play this role. Whatever a nonprofit decides, it has to be clear who is in charge. Mixed messages, poor communication, and lack of trust can hurt the effectiveness of the designated campaign leader and will ultimately undermine the fundraising effort.

Increasingly, as campaigns become more complex, larger, and last longer, the chief advancement officer also functions as an institutional leader and senior officer in the nonprofit, with substantial input into setting institutional priorities, strategic planning, and board composition and membership. In response to this enhanced role, many development professionals at the top of their field now have MBAs or advanced coursework in nonprofit management to help them serve their organizations in ways that go beyond the raising of funds.

Volunteer Leadership

It is important to have volunteers involved in various aspects of the campaign, particularly in outreach to other prospects in their communities. Some campaign directors have moved so completely to the staff-driven model that volunteers have become less engaged in the work and the success of the campaign. While it is undeniably true that volunteers can take lots of staff time to manage and support, dropping them altogether can be harmful to the organization. In managing a campaign, you always have to keep one eye on the future, and the more advocates of your mission you can create during the campaign, the better your organization will be served in years to come.

Campaign Volunteer Structure

The capital campaign committee is the most common volunteer structure used to support the work of a capital campaign. The committee can be big or small, with 5 to 50 members, and it can elect one chairman or many co-chairs. How

An elderly woman who had never married inherited a substantial family fortune. She became involved in a nonprofit organization to which she made generous annual contributions. As her health deteriorated over a period of several years, members of the development staff took to making regular visits to her home to keep her company and update her on their activities.

After her death, the nonprofit was thrilled to discover that she had left them a large gift in her will. Unfortunately, however, her nephew filed suit, claiming that the staff of the nonprofit had exerted undue influence over her during the period in which her health and mind had deteriorated before her death. As proof, the nephew offered video-taped evidence of members of the staff going in and out of his aunt's house periodically during her illness.

Although the nonprofit sought to fight the allegations in court, their lawyers advised them to settle. They ultimately did so, losing a portion of the bequest to the nefarious nephew.

often the committee meets depends on the work to be done; some meet weekly, some meet monthly, and some meet only twice a year. Because campaigns recruit volunteers who are very busy in their own lives, and may be spread out all over the country, meeting by conference call is always an option.

Large national campaigns find it useful to develop several tiers of volunteer structures based on region, area of responsibility, and affiliation. A university or a national organization, for instance, might want to identify regional campaign chairs, and create regional committees, and may even provide regional staff to support the work of regional volunteers (see Exhibit 4.4).

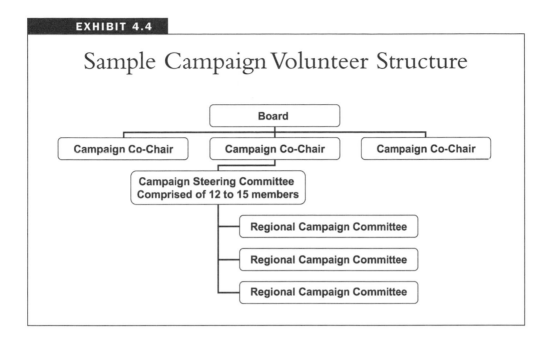

EXHIBIT 4.4

Sample Campaign Volunteer Structure

A smaller nonprofit operating in one region might want to keep the structure simpler, with one committee and one chair. An alternative model for the small shop is to diversify by identifying three co-chairs, selecting one co-chair who is in charge of corporate prospects, one who concentrates on wealthy individuals, and one who is focused on foundation activity. In general, having more chairs means that your campaign can reach more prospects.

Five Reasons to Have Several Co-Chairs instead of One Campaign Chair:

1. More chairs can reach more prospects.

2. One chair can burn out from carrying too much of the workload.

3. Co-chairs who share the responsibility lead to better problem solving.

4. Co-chairs from different backgrounds can appeal to different prospects.

5. More chairs with "big names" can impress prospective donors.

TIPS & TECHNIQUES

Qualities to Look for in a Campaign Chair:

- Capacity to make a leadership gift

- Ability to lead others

- Time and energy to commit to the campaign

- Loyalty and passion for the organization and its mission

- Experience asking for gifts

- Recognizable name that is respected in the community

EXHIBIT 4.5

Sample Job Description: Campaign Chair or Co-Chair

1. Provide leadership for all campaign activities.

2. Plan your own gift commensurate with the resources available.

3. Chair meetings of the campaign committee (identify frequency).

4. Allow the use of your name and position in campaign materials.

5. Host and attend campaign events, such as the campaign kick-off.

6. Identify and open the door to prospects for the campaign.

7. Assist with the cultivation and solicitation of top prospects.

8. Serve on the steering committee for the campaign.

EXHIBIT 4.6

Sample Job Description:
Campaign Committee Member

1. Support the capital campaign through your personal efforts.

- Our goal is to have 100% participation in gifts for the campaign from members of the board and the campaign committee.

- Plan your own gift to the campaign within your means.

- Contribute to the campaign in other nonfinancial ways, such as hosting an event, contributing professional services, or committing time.

2. Serve as an ambassador for the organization.

- Allow your name to be listed as a committee member in printed materials.

- Attend meetings of the campaign committee (specify frequency).

- Serve on the host committee for campaign events and attend when possible.

- Assist with public relations outreach and related communication efforts.

3. Assist with the identification and solicitation of prospects.

- Help identify potential prospects whom you know or can reach.

- Assist in determining the best way to approach the prospects you know.

- Be willing to open the door for staff, volunteers, or board members to call on prospects whom you know.

- Make solicitation calls as a member of a team representing the organization.

Steering committees can also be a helpful addition to the campaign volunteer structure. A steering committee composed of three campaign co-chairs, the board chair, and the president or executive director could meet regularly to set policy, plan activity, and assign prospects to a larger campaign committee that meets less often.

Recruiting volunteers can be done by staff or the committee chair. It should always be clear to a volunteer what you are asking them to do, who they will work with, and how their work fits into the bigger scheme of the campaign. In recruiting a volunteer, try to meet with her face to face, in order to be able to assess her skill level and answer her questions thoroughly. Prepare a formal job description that outlines the position, the duties, the term of service, and the expectations (see Exhibits 4.5 and 4.6).

Volunteer Training

Giving campaign volunteers meaningful work that they are prepared to do is the key to their success. *Remember that a volunteer is not an effective fundraiser until she has made her own gift to the campaign.*

Most campaigns involve their volunteers in the actual process of fundraising, that is, the identification, cultivation, and solicitation of prospects. The most productive way to use campaign volunteers is to tap into their knowledge of the prospective donor community. This might involve literally reviewing their Rolodex or Palm Pilot in order to create an invitation list for an event, or it could be asking them to make follow-up calls on key prospects to ask them for a gift.

Many volunteers, even experienced campaigners, need some support and training when it comes to asking for money. Organizations can provide formal training sessions for campaign volunteers. Such a session can help put volunteers at ease, shows the volunteers that the organization supports their efforts, and often creates bonds among members of the committee who will be working together over the course of the campaign. Sessions can be run by a member of the non-profit's advancement team, by a consultant, or by an experienced volunteer.

A training session also gives the organization an opportunity to teach its volunteers how to talk about more complex giving arrangements, such as planned gifts, stock gifts, and long-term pledges. An important side effect of such training is that the volunteers themselves start thinking about their own giving plans.

Training volunteers to ask can also be accomplished informally, simply by pairing them with a more experienced solicitor or including them as a member of a team on calls to prospective donors. Ask a volunteer to open the door to a prospect whom she knows, then bring her along with an experienced solicitor or staff member on the call. The volunteer should be assigned a specific role in advance that she is comfortable with, such as expressing why she supports the organization. As the volunteer observes the other members of the solicitation team, she is learning how to play the role of solicitor in the next meeting.

Some of the tasks that volunteers are effective doing don't require additional training or staff support. For instance, some volunteers can provide free or at-cost assistance to the campaign in their own areas of professional expertise, such as public relations, communications, banking, bond underwriting, investment practices, event planning, entertainment, tech support, video production, computer equipment, or catering.

Staffing and Tracking of Volunteer Activity

In today's more complex campaigns, where each staff member may be managing hundreds of prospects and numerous volunteers, it is imperative to have a prospect management system that works. In the old days, campaign staff kept index cards in a box under each volunteer's name, with prospect information and activity on each card. In the world of electronic information systems, even a small campaign can track prospect assignments and activity through Excel spreadsheets or a database maintained on a laptop.

When campaigns lose their ability to staff and track volunteer activity, big problems arise. Professional campaigners love to tell horror stories of volunteers run amok, calling on each others' prospects, making promises that the organization can't fulfill, asking prospects worth millions for a token gift of $10,000, unintentionally insulting donors, and generally providing such a poor public image for the organization that it can take years to erase the harm done.

Deal with the problem before it occurs by managing volunteers effectively from the beginning. Campaign volunteers should be working with an assigned staff member who stays in close touch, knows what they are doing, knows who they are calling on, and provides research and back-up support for all their calls. If volunteers begin to act inappropriately, call in the campaign leadership to help bring order. Ultimately, although it can be difficult to do, firing a volunteer is preferable to permanently harming the relationships being built with potential supporters.

Larger organizations now purchase sophisticated database management tools that are designed specifically for prospect management. There are many on the market that can be configured to match your current prospect information system. Be sure to plan and conduct training sessions for your advancement staff on the system that you implement.

Whatever system you choose, make sure that it works for your organization's level of technical capability and that people will use it. Spending thousands of dollars on a prospect management system doesn't help if no one fills in the required fields. Make it clear that all activity needs to be identified and tracked on the system by internal staff before you begin working with outside volunteers.

Summary

Campaigns require the integrated efforts of board members, advancement staff, the executive director, volunteers, and the campaign leadership in order to succeed. Board leadership is the most important component in setting the pace for involve-

TIPS & TECHNIQUES

Prospect Information That Should Be Tracked in Your System:

- Name, address, and contact information for the prospect

- Prospect affiliation, such as corporation or foundation, with address

- Volunteer(s) assigned to the prospect

- Gift rating, or capacity, for the prospect to give to this campaign

- Readiness of the prospect for a solicitation

- Giving interest area for the prospect

- Recent past activities undertaken with prospect, with date and result

- Next steps, or future activity planned for the prospect, with dates

- Staff member responsible for managing the activity of the prospect

ment, gifts, and leadership. Professional development staff members and executive directors have become more involved in asking for money but many campaigns still find that having volunteers involved in prospect cultivation and solicitation serves both the campaign and the long-term good of the organization.

Volunteer use can be organized effectively through campaign committees, the use of volunteer job descriptions, and careful staff management. Training volunteers is an essential part of good volunteer management. Good campaign management requires detailed tracking and planning of prospect activity, often with the assistance of new computerized prospect management systems. If all of these components function smoothly, the campaign will reach more people more efficiently.

Working with Volunteers:
The Capital Campaign Committee

A small, community nonprofit had a wonderful and committed board of grassroots supporters, but they didn't have any individuals of wealth among them. The organization needed a new facility and the board decided to mount a capital campaign to raise $750,000. This amount was way beyond their expertise and financial capacity, and they had no professional fundraising staff. How to proceed?

The executive director hired a fundraising consultant to plan and run the campaign. Several members of the board agreed to help identify and recruit a group of new volunteers of greater wealth and influence who were asked to form a capital campaign committee. All the new committee members were also strongly committed to the mission of the organization.

One of the new committee members offered to host an event in his home and pay for it as a method of attracting prospective donors. The other members contributed names for the invitation list and made phone calls to get people there. After the event, a team of three, including the consultant, the executive director, and one of the committee members, made follow-up calls on the event attendees and asked for gifts.

This model was repeated successfully several times. Within 18 months the goal was reached.

CHAPTER 5

Making a Compelling Case

 After reading this chapter, you will be able to:

- Build your campaign case statement.
- Develop outstanding campaign materials.
- Make your case through electronic media.

Building Your Case Statement

Building the case for your campaign is an important function that is directly tied to your ability to motivate donors to contribute to your campaign. The case is no more or less than the basic argument for why someone should contribute. Most campaigns develop short versions and long versions of the case for different uses. Some of those versions are published in an attractive and expensive format with photos, charts, and graphs; others may be used simply in desktop versions or as one component of a larger grant proposal.

Who Should Develop the Case Statement?

Many organizations write their case in-house. There are advantages to keeping this function in-house; your staff knows your strengths, mission, and vision better than anyone else, and your writer may already be familiar with your donors. Internal choices for the writer depend on the skills and availability of the people involved: consider the development staff writer, the chief advancement officer, or the PR director. In some organizations, the executive director or president writes the case to ensure that it matches her vision.

Another popular option is to hire a publications firm, marketing firm, or consultant to work on your case statement. An external writer may help you end up with fresher copy, a more logical flow to your prose, and new ways of positioning your organization to attract support. Make sure that the chief advancement officer and the staff who will be responsible for marketing the campaign have input and control over the ultimate content and form of the case if it is written outside the organization, or it may not be designed to fit your needs.

If you do decide to work with a consultant, have the writer spend time with members of your organization and learn what makes your nonprofit unique and special. Set up small focus groups to discuss how your constituents feel about the services you provide. Brainstorm with your most creative staff members and consultants about how to best capture the sense of where the future of the organization lies.

Link the Case to Your Mission and Vision

The basic concept behind making the case for your campaign is to show how the project for which you are fundraising will improve your organization's ability to meet its mission in the future. The visionary aspect comes with the interplay of future needs with the present limitations, that is, how well you can project your organization's needs into the future and show that they will be met in a timely, creative, and enlightened manner.

Focus your case by coming up with two or three key themes that you want your target audience to be aware of. For instance, in the example case in Exhibit 5.1, for an art museum expansion campaign, the museum director decided on two key themes: educational outreach to schoolchildren (their district was cutting back on art funding in schools), and the positive economic impact of two blockbuster exhibits the museum had mounted over the past three years.

Marketing 101: Test and Target Your Case

Basic marketing concepts can be very helpful to nonprofits in putting together a strong case. The selection of the key themes for your case statement is made during the planning period of the campaign. In order to help identify the themes that will resonate with your donors, pose a series of questions:

- Why do people support us now?
- What are we perceived as having done well in the past?
- What are the best arguments we can make for future support?
- How can we support those arguments with facts?

Test these questions with focus groups or small gatherings of supporters to learn whether your initial gut reactions are shared by others. You may want to ask your marketing or PR firm to help with such testing to keep it objective. Consider holding sessions with three different groups: staff, current donors, and nondonors. Zero in on several themes that get repeated by all the various constituencies of your organization.

If your organization has an identified constituency of supporters, such as members or alumni, you can use the campaign planning as a time to conduct a broad survey. Tell your alumni that you are planning a campaign, tell them that you want their advice, and ask them to tell you what, in their perception, you are doing well and not so well. Their opinions can help you shape both the reality and the marketing of your future plans and needs.

EXHIBIT 5.1

Sample Outline for a Case Statement: Art Museum Expansion Campaign

1. *Letter from the Chairman:*

- Introduces two key themes
  - Economic development
  - Education programs for elementary school children
- Identifies urgency of needs
  - Cites results of recent economic impact study
  - Emphasizes cuts to arts programs in public schools

2. *Brief History of the Museum:*

- Historical emphasis on community and inclusiveness
- Recent successes
  - Economic impact of the exhibits on the community
  - Programs for school children to see the exhibits

3. *Future Plans:*

- The need for expansion
  - Supports educational outreach with new classroom wing
  - Increased draw of out-of-town visitors, adding economic value
- Architectural plans
  - Rendering of new wing
  - Printing new floor plans in format easy for laypersons to read

4. *Campaign Details at a Glance:*

- Campaign leadership and committee (list by name)
- Naming opportunities and prices
- Campaign timetable
- Contact information
- Ways to give: cash, pledge, planned gift information

TIPS & TECHNIQUES

Tie your capital campaign to a theme that is linked to your mission:

Campaign Purpose	Theme
Expanding art museum	Educational outreach to schoolchildren
New science wing	Environmentally friendly construction plan
New community center	Adult literacy and economic development
Endowment campaign	Educate and serve future generations
New school building	Educated workforce
Community arts center	Job training and tourism
Hospital expansion	Health care for the aging population

Don't hesitate to share outside views generated through focus groups or surveys with your board and other decision makers, even if they are negative. Different ways of looking at your organization, its successes, and its challenges should be viewed as helpful, not threatening.

Targeting the message to different market segments is also a basic marketing tool that can work well in the nonprofit world. A simple analysis of your donor constituency will probably show very different segments of donors: corporations, foundations, individuals, and local and out-of-town donors will all be represented. Think about refining your case to appeal to different segments of donors.

For instance, local donors might be very interested in the economic impact of your expansion in your community, whereas donors from outside your state might be completely indifferent to this theme. Consider writing two different versions of your case statement, one that emphasizes local economic impact issues, and another that focuses on the national need for organizations like yours.

Components of the Case Statement

Most printed case statements are multipaged brochures that begin with an introductory section on the history of the nonprofit organization, the mission statement, and a brief summary of recent successes. Often charts, timetables, pull quotes, and personal statements from the organization's leaders are used in this section to keep the reader involved and make the printed page look more interesting. A letter from the chairman of the board, the campaign chair, or the executive director also can add a personal touch to the basic introductory information.

The second section develops the themes for the campaign, explains the reasons why the funds are needed, and shares the vision for where the organization is headed. Think of the heading for this section as "Why Invest in This Organization Now?" This section needs to be emotionally compelling and create a sense of urgency, but it should also include enough facts to make the campaign feel real. Personal comments and stories from users and beneficiaries of the nonprofit's services can be effective tools in communicating the themes in this section.

A third section deals with the details of the project being funded by the campaign. This portion might include floor plans, architectural renderings, project descriptions, and site plans. The more visual you can make the presentation of your campaign needs the better. Many prospects do not get excited about capital projects unless they can visualize what the project will look like. It is worth the money to have your architects and designers produce high-quality visual materials for inclusion in your case statement.

There is a variety of other information that can be included in the case, such as a list of all your board members; a list of the capital campaign committee members; the Table of Needs with prices and naming opportunities; the campaign goal and timetable; and giving information, such as contact names and types of gifts that the campaign will accept.

Some campaigns print two versions of the case statement, a full one for calls on top potential donors, and a shorter, inexpensive version for use with visitors, direct mail, and lower-level donors. You can adjust your materials depending on the phase of the campaign: for the quiet phase, print a small number of expensive case pieces; print more copies of another version later for the public phase. Using a new version in the public phase can provide the opportunity to update goals and the total funds raised, and sharpen the case based on early reactions from donors.

Develop Outstanding Campaign Materials

What Materials Does Your Organization Need?

It might seem that campaigns require a lot of materials, contributing to the high cost of the preparation and execution of the fundraising plan (see Exhibit 5.2). Hundreds of thousands of dollars can be budgeted and spent for printed brochures, videos, logo design, and four-color renderings of architectural mas-

LIVE & LEARN

A private charitable foundation was established upon the death of a philanthropist who had designed and built parking garages, among other things, for a living. The foundation soon made a major donation to the man's alma mater to build and endow a parking garage. Parking is a major issue on every urban campus, and the gift was received with great enthusiasm.

When the garage was built and dedicated, a parking space at the entrance was reserved for the deceased donor, marked with an engraved brass plaque. The parking space remains empty *in perpetuity* out of respect to the foresight and generosity of a loyal graduate.

terpieces. The truth is, however, that often the self-image of the president, the public image desired by the organization, and the campaign needs become intertwined, and many nonprofits produce expensive materials that aren't necessary to deliver the gifts needed.

Campaign materials have three main goals: to educate, to persuade, and to help the nonprofit stand out from the competition. Education, the first goal, is relatively straightforward, and answers the questions: What does your organization do? Why is it important? Brochures, written proposals, videos, and PowerPoint presentations can all be used appropriately to make these points. In general, high-quality writing and strong, stirring personal stories will carry your educational efforts farther than glossy brochures.

The second goal, to persuade, also can be supported by quality written and visual aids. The question the donor is asking is: Why should I make a gift to your organization? Pictures, individual stories of people's needs being met, and the high emotional impact of film or video all can be used to convey the urgency of your needs. It is rare, however, for major gifts to be pledged on the basis of the donor reviewing materials alone. In most cases, the decision to make a gift is heavily influenced by personal solicitations. The personal elements of a solicitation—who does the asking, and what they ask for—often carry more weight than any brochures or video you present.

Finally, there remains the goal of uniqueness, of how your organization can stand out in a crowded field of nonprofits, all of whom have urgent needs. Here again both the quality and content of the campaign materials can set the organization off from its peers. With skillful design work, the campaign can be

RULES OF THE ROAD

Take credit when things go well, because you will get
the blame when they don't.

set off with a unique look; for instance, an attractive logo or bold color group-ing that can be repeated in all the materials may help the campaign stand out from the competition.

Experienced solicitors often call on a prospect without much in the way of supporting materials, with the confidence that their personal call is enough to

---

EXHIBIT 5.2

Materials for a $150 Million Capital Campaign

- Fifteen-page printed book: full case statement
- Fourfold printed brochure: small case statement
- Eight-minute campaign video (VHS and/or DVD format)
- Campaign stationery with list of campaign committee
- Color copies of architectural renderings
- Copies of press releases and PR coverage
- Campaign event invitation template
- Campaign proposal templates
- Price list for naming opportunities (printed on desktop so it can be changed and updated)
- Printed pocket folder to hold proposals and other materials
- Quarterly newsletter
- Direct-mail pieces with campaign themes and renderings
- Planned giving brochure
- PowerPoint presentation on campaign needs and goals
- Notebook for campaign volunteers

---

persuade the donor. On the other hand, with inexperienced volunteers, the quality and nature of campaign materials can contribute to their gaining confidence on a call. The quality of materials can also be self-fulfilling, that is, high-quality materials can persuade the donor that the organization is of a high quality, and that therefore the campaign is important and worthy of support.

Campaign Materials on a Tight Budget

There is a strong argument to be made for simplifying campaign materials and spending less on campaign costs overall (see Exhibit 5.3). Most donors don't want their gifts to be spent on elaborate publications. Almost any donor, given the choice, would prefer that his gift be spent on furthering the project, program, or mission of the nonprofit organization. Some donors vociferously object to expensive, glossy print publications as wasteful and unnecessary.

The use of electronic materials can be a boon for organizations on a tight budget. Now, with the widespread availability of digital cameras, desktop publishing, PowerPoint presentations, CD burners, and color printers, you can make your campaign look very professional with a minimal amount of money spent on printing, paper, and outside design work.

How professional your materials will look depends a lot on how experienced your staff is in using these tools. If you don't have the skills in-house, ask your volunteers or board members if they can help. Ask for contributions, trade-outs, or special deals with printers, designers, and Web developers. Remember, money saved on campaign materials can go directly into your project's budget.

Making the Case through Electronic Media

PowerPoint Presentations

PowerPoint has become a relatively easy medium to master, and it provides any size organization with an inexpensive opportunity to make a strong, visually

---

EXHIBIT 5.3

Materials for a $2 Million Capital Campaign (On a Tight Budget)

- Print four-page brochure: minicase statement (all writing and digital photography supplied in-house; design and printing bid out; paper donated).

- Create PowerPoint presentation in-house (using images and design elements from case statement).

- Purchase pocket folders in a complementary color.

- Make color copies of PR articles from local newspaper.

- Create desktop logo.

- Print stationery and invitations in-house using color printer.

- Create desktop proposal templates and pricing lists.

- Create campaign page on Web site with video of recent events.

- Personalize PowerPoint presentations with name of donor.

- Burn presentation on a CD and design label with logo in-house.

---

effective presentation. The medium can work well in front of a single donor, using a laptop, or with a group, using a projector. The presentation can also be burned onto a CD for use at many different functions.

A PowerPoint presentation, like a printed case statement, should be focused, easy to understand, and visually compelling. Unlike a printed piece, however, it is inexpensive and easy to update, and can be personalized without additional cost. A presentation using an electronic format can also make your

Uses for a PowerPoint Presentation:

- Make it part of the program at an event, such as a reception.

- Keep it available in your conference room for visitors.

- Send it ahead of a meeting with prospects.

- Use it during a personal meeting with a prospect.

- Leave behind a copy after your visit.

- Send it with a thank-you.

- Make the images available on your Web site.

organization seem more up to date in our digital age. If you are meeting with a prospective donor in his or her home or office, however, you will need to bring along or locate the necessary equipment, either a laptop or projector, depending on the size of the group and the nature of the visit.

There are some useful rules for these kinds of presentations. Don't try to do too much in one show; generally speaking, plan for 15 to 20 slides for a 15-minute presentation. And don't read each line of the slide copy, which can be annoying and repetitive. Instead, select one item from the slide copy to comment further on, or make a summary statement that covers all the facts on the slide. Count on about one minute per slide and practice with a colleague so that you can time your presentation appropriately.

Any organization with a minimum of technological support can personalize each presentation, burn a CD, and present it to the prospective donor. Consider putting the name of the company or individual you are soliciting on the cover, the first slide, and the slide where you ask for a gift. You can also list the specific gift levels and the recognition you will be offering using the prospect's name. Leave behind a copy of the presentation for members of the prospect's family, foundation board, or company who were not able to join you during your visit.

Campaign Web Sites

Many campaigns now support their outreach to their constituents with additional information on their Web sites. Some large organizations create a new Web site for their capital campaigns with a link from their main site. Others add a page, or pages, to their main site with a link or banner on the home page. Your needs will depend on your assessment of how many hits your Web site gets, how you will drive additional traffic to the site during your campaign, and how interactive you intend your campaign site to become.

Interactive Web sites are a good way to engage and involve potential donors, especially younger and older people. Most Web use research shows that users cluster in two groups: those under 40, especially Generation Xers in their late twenties and thirties, and older, retired people who have the time, money, and interest to pursue Web-related activities. You will want to think about what groups you are trying to engage when you plan your Web site.

Interactivity can be related to your mission and outreach; for instance, volunteers can sign up on the Web, Web users can access additional educational materials, or art lovers can peruse a museum's collection at leisure on-line. Many organizations now include photos that are capable of being easily downloaded or used as wallpaper for a user's PC, updated news and PR items, and links to related sites. Chat rooms, on-line event planning, and the on-line sale of branded items are all growing methods of utilizing electronic communication to tie users to your organization.

Web sites can also be designed to directly support fundraising efforts. Perhaps the most obvious is building in the capability for a donor to make a gift or buy a membership on-line. Commercial products are now available that blend seamlessly into an organization's Web site and provide interactive fundraising information for complex tools such as planned giving. Calculators to provide information on trusts and annuities have become one popular method of providing interactivity with potential planned-giving donors.

Another fast-growing use of Web sites in campaign fundraising involves donor recognition and advertising. Corporations, foundations, and individuals are being offered Web site recognition on lists for giving at specific levels; banners, ads, and live links on nonprofit Web sites are being offered as part of corporate sponsorship packages. How involved your organization becomes in such advertising activities is a decision that combines elements of good taste, the nature of your mission, and community standards.

Videos, CD-ROMs, and Other Media Presentations

As multimedia tools proliferate, it is becoming easier and less expensive for an organization to create memorable presentations. Videos have been around for years, and many educational institutions use them for recruiting prospective students. Fundraising videos can be more problematic, because the organization must decide exactly how they will be used.

Video, like film, can be a very powerful medium. The combination of music, pictures, action, and script can provide an emotionally moving experience for your viewers. Unscripted segments featuring people who visit your organization or who benefit from your services can also provide great emotional impact. In general, try to avoid having the video dominated by "talking heads," such as your president, board chair, and others who may feel that their image is a key component of your media efforts. Try to break up speechifying about your organization with natural shots of people using your services or short informal interviews with actual service providers.

TIPS & TECHNIQUES

Questions to Ask When Planning a Campaign Video:

- How will this be used with the prospect—as part of a personal meeting, as a leave-behind, or as a piece to be mailed separately?

- Does the video need to stand alone, or will it be paired with the case statement, brochures, or other materials?

- Do you want to ask for money in the video?

- How much do you want to spend?

- What do you want someone to feel after seeing it?

- What do you want someone to do after seeing it?

- Will there be a separate follow-up mechanism?

- Is this video appropriate to make available on the Web site?

Fundraising can be approached in direct or indirect ways in a campaign video, depending on how you want to present your needs to prospective donors. Some fundraising videos don't actually address fundraising; rather, they make their case by engaging the viewer directly and emotionally in the day-to-day work of the organization.

A community job training center, for instance, might film a sequence in which three or four people who have found jobs through the center relate their experiences in a personal manner, much like visual storytelling. One advantage of this mode of presentation is that the video, since it doesn't include a direct fundraising ask, can be used for multiple purposes by the organization, such as recruiting staff, PR, public events, motivational meetings, and so forth.

Most campaign videos, however, are geared directly toward educating the prospective donor about the nonprofit's long-term needs and motivating the viewer to make a gift to support those needs. Some campaign videos open or close with an appeal by the campaign chair, particularly if the chair is well-known or charismatic. This is a good way to use a celebrity chair, for instance.

Other videos include interviews with articulate donors talking about why they made a gift in support of the effort. Tying a donor with the recipient, such as showing a scholarship recipient talking with the donor of an endowed scholarship, is one way to link the cause and effect of philanthropy in a visual manner. Capital campaign videos usually also include an introduction to the architectural plans or renderings of a proposed facility, with an explanation about the need for the facility as part of the organization's future plans.

With the advent of new technology, it is now possible to use CD-ROMs to make virtual images of future buildings, rotate and "enter" architectural plans, and create 3-D images of futuristic campuses complete with sound and graphic details. While some of these options may require a level of technical sophistication that is very expensive, many donors enjoy the "wow" factor in these presentations. Just like advertisements, campaign materials have to be able to cut through the clutter of complicated lives in order to be effective.

It also may be important to your institution to be on the cutting edge of available technology. For example, if you work for a science museum or a research-level university, using the latest technology may be an important factor in positioning your institution among your competitors. You need to show donors that you can produce a highly sophisticated presentation because it reflects the sophistication of your product. If so, plan to spend a larger portion of your budget on electronic support materials.

Summary

The materials used to present the case for a capital campaign need to match the mission, vision, budget, and needs of the organization. Campaign materials can be as sophisticated, complex, and expensive as you desire them to be; many options now exist for creating desktop materials that are lively, colorful, inexpensive, and flexible to use. Technology can be a useful tool in supplementing outreach to various constituencies, including the use of CD-ROMs, PowerPoint, video, and Web sites to help carry your message and case to your audience.

CHAPTER 6

Prospect Identification, Cultivation, and Solicitation

After reading this chapter, you will be able to:

- Expand your prospect list.
- Create a cultivation process for prospects.
- Ask for and close major gifts.

Expanding Your Prospect List

Now that you have the plan and the volunteer structure for your capital campaign completed, you need campaign prospects. How do names of potential prospects surface? What is the difference between suspects and qualified prospects? Can your organization find substantial new sources of donors? The answers to these questions lie in creating a dedicated, rigorous prospect research function in your organization.

Conducting Prospect Research

Prospect research has matured from scribbling index cards in the file room to a recognized professional career path. The function should have a dedicated full-time or part-time staff member in the advancement operation whose time, expertise, and training are focused on prospect research. With the advent of new Web-searching technology, a fully stocked research library may not be required, but an adequate budget for staff and electronic resources is a must.

Prospect research is both a science and an art. As in any scientific endeavor, the researcher must have a true understanding of what he or she is looking for, including knowing how to recognize the profile of a likely donor, what areas of interest coincide with donors to the organization, and how to research the financial details of corporate and personal wealth.

The art, however, comes into play with the researcher's ability to follow a minor thread, to intuitively follow the path of a prospect's public life and interests

 TIPS & TECHNIQUES

Why Conduct Prospect Research?

- To identify new prospects

- To determine the giving capacity of prospects once they are identified

- To help determine the best strategy for approaching a prospect

- To provide relevant information to your solicitors before a call

- To learn more about current donors to your organization

- To identify giving patterns and help build bridges to new constituencies in order to determine if a good match exists between the prospect and the organization's needs. Sometimes small details are critical, for instance, discovering that a prospect for a hospital cancer wing expansion had a mother who died from breast cancer. Both training and instinct underlie the work of an experienced prospect researcher.

There are many fertile sources of names for campaign prospect lists (see Exhibit 6.1). Start with those who are closest to you—past and current donors to your organization. Don't forget alumni, grateful patients, visitors, or those who have experienced positive benefits from your services. Assign someone to read the local papers, including business weeklies, and to clip articles with an eye to your donor pool. Invest in some electronic search capabilities, such as Lexis Nexis and one of the foundation search engines. Consider running your current donor list through an electronic prospect research service. And plan an organized method of pursuing a proven method of identifying likely prospects—asking your board, campaign committee, and other volunteers for names.

Once you begin tapping into these sources, you soon will be overwhelmed with names and will need to find ways to screen, prioritize, and rate prospects as you acquire them. Two tried-and-true methods of organizing prospect names are by *capacity, or rating, and by closeness, or familiarity with your organization.* You can use both of these systems together to help prioritize your prospect list by ranking those who can make the biggest gifts and those who are most likely to give at the top of your list.

To make the first cut, sort your prospects by capacity. Begin by identifying the lowest gift level that you want to consider as a major gift to your campaign. Campaigns should identify a major gift level based on the total campaign goal and the history of giving to the organization. Smaller nonprofits that have never conducted a campaign may consider $5,000 or $10,000 to be a major gift; larger, more experienced organizations will set a higher major gift level, from $25,000 to $100,000.

EXHIBIT 6.1

Sources of Potential Campaign Prospects

- Names given by board members, campaign committee members, and other key volunteers

- Current donors to your annual fund or other programs

- Current members

- Past donors to your organization

- Lists of donors to groups with a similar mission

- Users of your organization's services (alumni, prior patients, visitors, parents of students, those who benefit from your programs)

- Community leaders and major philanthropists in your city

- Foundations that support other groups active in your field

- Corporations that support other groups active in your field

- Local business lists (many business newspapers provide CD-ROMs of local corporations, including officers' names and contact info)

- Newspapers (clip articles on philanthropists, gift announcements, social pages, business sections, and special-event coverage)

- List acquisition (go through a reputable list broker and test different mailing lists before purchasing large lists)

- List bartering (trade membership or donor lists with another organization that has a mission similar to yours)

- Web site (create a place for visitors to your Web site to leave their name and contact information)

Consider this gift level as the floor for your major gift prospect list and start screening for prospects who can make *at least* a gift of that level. After the appropriate research is completed, assign each major gift prospect a capacity rating, for the highest-level gift you think they could make to your campaign if they were properly cultivated.

Rate donors by assigning them to standard giving ranges, such as $10,000 to $25,000; $25,000 to $50,000; $50,000 to $100,000; $100,000 to $250,000; and $250,000 to $500,000. Make sure that these rating levels match the ranges that you have identified in your gift table (see Chapter 2). Your ultimate goal is to have enough prospects identified, with ratings assigned, to fill up your gift table. You don't need to have all the names at every level filled in at the beginning of your campaign, because as you reach out to new prospects, new volunteers, and new constituencies, your prospect list will expand.

If you find that the top end of your giving range is sparsely populated with prospect names at the beginning of your campaign, this can be a danger sign that you are being too aggressive in setting the top-level gift amounts. Your campaign might need to raise more gifts at lower levels, where most of your prospects are congregated. This will require adjusting your gift table, which is often done after the early stages of a campaign. Don't forget that you will need three to four prospects for each gift realized in each gift range.

There are many factors to consider in determining giving capacity:

- Research the prospect's giving to other organizations. Try to determine the largest gift and the average gift she has made to other nonprofits.

- Assess the net worth of this prospect; include income, assets, homes, investments, stockholdings, and so on.

- Ask peers who know the prospect and who are connected with your organization to help you estimate the prospect's giving potential.

- Assess the impact of lifestyle changes on the prospect's wealth, such as divorce, retirement, illness, children attending college, and inheritance.

- Factor in any changes in the valuation of the source of the prospect's wealth, such as changes in stock value or a new contract for a closely held company.

- For an individual, research whether they have set up a family foundation or perhaps created a fund at a community foundation.

- For a foundation, use one of the on-line foundation directories to determine giving levels, interest areas, trustees, and application procedures.

A second variable to consider is how close each prospect is to your organization. Review such aspects as whether the prospect already is or has been a donor to your cause; whether they have visited you, or are known personally to you or a member of your volunteer team; and whether they have a known affinity to your mission or area of service. Create a simple rating system, such as a 1-to-5 scale, with 1 being extremely close (such as a current board member) and 5 being distant (such as someone who is known to be philanthropic but whom you have never met). Apply these ratings to help track your progress with prospects over the course of the campaign.

LIVE & LEARN

A longtime supporter of a nonprofit passed away, leaving his beloved stable of polo ponies to the charity. The officials at the charity rejoiced in their knowledge that the ponies were very valuable and would fetch a great price at sale.

Unfortunately it took months to settle the estate, arrange for the sale of the ponies, and deliver them to their new owners. Meanwhile, the ponies required expensive care, grooming, and feeding. After all their costs, the charity actually realized only a small percentage of the ultimate value of the ponies.

Use your ratings system for giving capacity and closeness to prioritize and order your top prospects. When assigning prospects to volunteers, planning staff travel, inviting prospects to campaign events, or setting up personal meetings, always start at the top of the list with those who can give the most and who have the closest affinity to your organization. That way you will put the greatest effort into cultivating and soliciting those who can return the most to your campaign in the shortest possible time.

Volunteer Screening and Prospect Review

Good campaign volunteers are the key to the success of most capital campaigns. It is very important to learn as quickly and efficiently as possible who your volunteers know, who they can open doors to, and who they are willing to cultivate and solicit on your behalf. Organized, methodical prospect screening has become a function of both the research and the major gift staff members working together.

Prospect lists can be sorted by region, by alphabetical order, by past giving level to your organization, or by an assigned capacity rating. In universities, prospect review is usually done by class (linked to year of graduation and age) and geographic area of residence. Sorting prospects by city also would be useful for research hospitals, national museums, health-care groups, and other nationally based charitable organizations.

Be very careful to respect the confidentiality of your donors. Prospect lists that will be used for screening should not include personal giving information, nor should they identify rating levels that have been assigned by staff. Do not provide information that could unduly influence the outcome of a rating session, such as largest past gift.

Conducting Group Prospect Screening and Rating Sessions

Conducting a prospect screening session can be fun and can also serve as a cultivation for the participants at the beginning of the capital campaign planning period. Plan your list production carefully—this is the key to good prospect screening. Print out your lists with no more than a few hundred names for maximum ease of review.

Make plans to host screening sessions in major cities where you have supporters. Invite your participants to meet in a private room, such as a hotel conference center or someone's home. Invite those who are already close to you, including donors and campaign leaders, and tell them up front in the invitation letter what you are asking them to do.

When you open the meeting, carefully explain the confidential nature of the information and how it will be used. Ask the participants to rate the capacity of everyone they know on the lists, and provide checklists for different levels of giving capacity. Also provide a space for the participant to indicate if he wishes to be involved in the cultivation or solicitation of the prospect identified. An

RULES OF THE ROAD

Murphy's Law of Development: no matter how many times
you check the names of your top 10 donors in your annual report,
one of them will be spelled wrong.

open-ended page where you ask the participant to list any other prospects he knows can be a useful addition.

You can also use a few minutes of the session to update your constituents on campaign plans. This is the perfect place to use the PowerPoint or video that you have created for the campaign. Be sure to thank everyone after you get back to the office—some of your participants may become your best donors once the campaign gets underway!

Some capital campaign committees spend their first sessions screening prospect lists to help organize and focus the campaign planning efforts at an early stage. In these meetings volunteers are not only giving information to staff about prospects, they are also taking prospect assignments for action. Group screening efforts with campaign volunteers should involve an open discussion of strategy, decisions about who would be the best person to make a solicitation call, and sharing of new names with the advancement team.

Another method for acquiring information about prospects is to sit down in a one-on-one session with key volunteers and individual board members to review lists in a private setting. Any size organization can take advantage of this type of screening to maximize information gathering about top prospects and assist with prospect strategy and assignment.

Lists used in a personal screening session can be personalized to match the volunteer. Before the meeting, create a prospect list that includes names that match key traits of the volunteer, such as industry, religious affiliation, social circle, geographic residence, or profession. Ask a doctor to screen lists of other doctors, have an oil industry leader help strategize on involvement of other oil executives, review 50-year reunion lists with members of the 50-year reunion class, and so forth.

What should you do with all this information when you get back to the office? Many advancement information systems now have prospect-research modules that are designed to store and organize such information. Most organizations also keep paper files and store screening information by donor and prospect name. Others keep track of their prospect lists using Excel or a similar database. Your decision will depend on the capacity of your advancement office information system, your budget, the size of your prospect list, and the relative sophistication of your organization.

Electronic Prospect Research

Electronic research has now come of age. The Internet provides a wealth of resources for the trained prospect researcher (see Exhibit 6.2). Unfortunately,

LIVE & LEARN

A donor let it be known that he was interested in making the leadership gift to name a new building at a museum complex. When the museum officials sat down to discuss the details of the gift with him, he offered to donate stock in a new company that promised to extract gold from the sands of Africa. The stock value rose swiftly, then before the gift could be completed, it crashed, leaving the donor and many others reeling in the wake of an SEC investigation for fraud. The charity eventually gave the naming rights to another donor who produced a more saleable asset.

EXHIBIT 6.2

Resources for Prospect Research

Marquis *Who's-Who* listings

SEC data on stockholdings of insiders

Dun & Bradstreet private company data

Real estate holdings (from Lexis Nexis real estate or major mortgage holders)

Foundation directories (i.e., *Guidestar* or *The Foundation Directory*)

Lexis Nexis development universe

Standard & Poor's

Dow Jones

Hoovers

Edgars

Note: Most of these services have costs attached that are assessed either by individual use or subscription; some are redundant and not all will be required.

some of the best resources now come with a charge and others are time consuming to search and match with your organization's prospect names. You probably have learned to enter names into Google or a similar free search engine, but like many things in life, the quality of what you get is often related to how much you pay for it.

A wide range of for-profit firms now market electronic prospect screening solutions to nonprofits for capital campaign use. Most of these products compare the names in your database against publicly available information drawn from a wide variety of business and government databases. Some products augment the public information with closely held information or private databases they have purchased or maintained over a period of years. Their methods and sources differ, but their goal is to sell you specific information on your prospects by name, including information such as the value of stock holdings in public companies, private company ownership, real estate holdings, and gifts made to political campaigns. This kind of information can be very valuable in assessing the capacity of a donor to make a gift to your organization.

If you decide to contract with one of these services, be sure you know what you are buying and how you will use the information once you purchase it, because it can be very expensive. You may want to take advantage of the free test runs many of these companies offer so that you can see what the results would look like before purchasing a product. It is worth the time to compare similar products before you buy (see Exhibit 6.3).

The information provided by an electronic prospect-screening firm can add considerable value to your campaign. It is not intended to replace the advancement office researcher, but it can save your researcher time in bringing all the relevant sources together with one fast search engine. The results can help you prioritize top prospects within a large prospect pool. Some products now even provide relationship information; for example, linking a donor to your organization with a prospect with whom he serves on another nonprofit board.

There are many limitations to electronic research, and it should not be considered a panacea. It still takes a human being to sort, analyze, and make the research available to volunteers and staff in a coherent manner. An electronic prospect-research profile cannot tell you whether a donor will become passionate about your mission. Knowing the amount of stock a donor holds, and the value of that stock, does not hold the key to his heart or his pocket book. It can, however, help you determine the donor's capacity when you go to make your solicitation.

Don't take the human element out of development. Use research as one tool to inform the development process.

EXHIBIT 6.3

Service Providers:
Electronic Prospect-Screening Firms

Target America

Marts & Lundy

Bentz Whaley Flessner

Grenzebach Glier & Associates

Prospect Information Network (PIN)

Wealth ID

WealthEngine.com

MaGIC

Note: This is a partial list of firms that provide these services; it does not intend to rate, promote, or endorse any one firm over another.

The Process of Prospect Cultivation

Building Relationships

Anyone who has dealt with major gift fundraising, as opposed to fundraising through direct mail, telethons, and special events, knows that building personal relationships is the key to success. While all good relationships with prospective donors have elements that are unique to that individual and his or her interests, specific strategies for bringing relationships to a fruitful conclusion can be planned and applied to more than one prospect.

How long does it take to create a relationship that is strong enough to deliver a major gift to the organization? The answer can range from hours to a lifetime. Many great partnerships between a donor and an institution do last a lifetime, and include annual gifts, major gifts, and planned gifts. Some gifts of millions have been cemented in one personal visit with a prospect; others take years of cultivation. In general, leadership gifts of $1,000,000 and up take at least a year to 18 months to bring to the point of a written pledge document.

The development truism that *people give to people* is more important now than ever before. The relationship that exists between a major donor and a nonprofit should, at its best, transcend individuals within the organization, and be directly tied to the mission of the organization. Ideally, this allows the donor to maintain her tie to the nonprofit throughout changes in staffing and leadership. In reality, however, donors are often loyal to a specific individual's leadership, vision, and friendship, whether it is the executive director, the board chairman, or a major gifts staff member.

Patterns of Cultivation

Given the personal nature of the relationship between each donor and the institution, it may come as a surprise that it is possible to plan generic cultivation strategies within a capital campaign. Many organizations have developed flexible plans for cultivating prospects that identify a series of steps, or a process, of bringing the prospect closer to the organization and its realization of its mission. Exhibit 6.4 gives some examples of cultivation steps that can be planned for any prospective donor. How well you plan these steps will in turn determine how well your prospects respond to your case and your needs.

Note that each of these cultivation steps is indeed very personal, and each one helps to create a lasting tie between the prospect and the people she is meeting who are passionate about the cause. It is possible to select several of these steps, institutionalize them, and prioritize them in a series to develop a whole cadre of good relationships, *still highly personal,* with a number of prospective donors.

The point of a *cultivation process* is that it can be replicated with more than one donor, so that a system, or pattern, of developing relationships can be put in place for the campaign. The advantages of such a system are many: the results can be measured and quantified, the costs can be controlled, and staff support can be planned ahead of time. The best result is that, with repetition and practice, campaign volunteers, advancement staff members, and the executive director begin to establish a predictable style and rhythm in their interactions with prospective donors that makes the process fun, meaningful, and effective for all involved.

EXHIBIT 6.4

Examples of Cultivation Steps for a Major Prospective Donor

- Invite to a private dinner with the president or executive director.

- Invite to a small group dinner including peers who already support you.

- Bring the prospect in to see the new plans with the architect there.

- Write an article about the prospect that ties him in some way to your organization in your newsletter (get his permission first).

- Send a special gift or commemorative item from your organization.

- Bring the prospective donor in to meet personally with recipients who have benefited from the services that you provide.

- Set up a breakfast or lunch with the chairman of the board to view the campaign video and take a tour of your facilities.

- Visit the donor in his office; bring along the PowerPoint or campaign video.

- Nominate the prospect for an award or honor that you give out annually.

IN THE REAL WORLD

Planning the Cultivation Process

The advancement VP for a small art museum concluded that her best donors were those who visited the museum. It was difficult for her to cultivate and effectively solicit prospects who had never seen their collection. So she focused her cultivation strategies on steps that brought her best prospects to the museum a few at a time, where she and her director could give them plenty of personal attention. After some experimentation with scheduling, this is her plan. It is simple, flexible, makes effective use of a capital campaign volunteer, and it helped her to expand her donor base in her community:

1. She sends the prospective donor a special commemorative print from their last exhibit. It contains a note signed by a capital campaign committee member who knows him, telling him how important the museum is to the community and to the volunteer personally.

2. She has the volunteer call the prospect and invite him to a small group dinner with the museum president, several board members, and a few other prospective donors that includes a private tour of the new exhibit. He accepts and attends.

3. She and the director, accompanied by the volunteer, visit the prospective donor in his office and solicit him for a capital gift for their new expansion.

Making Contact: The Qualifying Call

Now that you have your prospect list, how do you zero in on those who are truly interested in your project? It's not very efficient to invite everyone on your list to have a personal dinner with the chairman of the board. The answer to help you prioritize and sort prospects is to make an introductory, or qualifying, call.

The qualifying call is a tried-and-true method of initiating contact with a prospective donor. It should be made by an advancement staff member, alone or with a volunteer. Wherever you got his name from—whether it be from another nonprofit's donor list, a campaign committee member, or a foundation directory—you want to test the waters first before sending in your chairman or your president. Don't feel you always have to open the door to a new prospect with your highest-level executive or chief volunteer; there will be time to meet the top people later in the cultivation process.

Using lower-level staff at the beginning of the relationship keeps things low-key, offers more opportunity to gain real information about the prospect, and allows for more efficient use of staff. It is important for the chief executive and board chair to focus their valuable time on prospects who are already qualified and ready to be asked for money. (An exception to this rule might be a truly top-level appointment, such as a meeting with Bill Gates or the CEO of Ford Motor Company, where you will have only one shot with the prospect and need to bring in all your big guns.)

The purpose of a qualifying call is twofold: first, to determine whether there is interest in the organization and the campaign; and second, to learn enough about the prospective donor to help you to determine what the next steps should be. Your first job is a sales job—you are selling your organization. You need to be prepared to make the case for your nonprofit, its purpose, mission, accomplishments, and future plans. Bring along whatever you think might help you accomplish this purpose—brochures, a video, or a volunteer, depending on their relationship with the prospect.

Always do your homework first, and be prepared to share any information you have with the volunteer who will accompany you. Determine if the prospect is a donor to similar causes; find out about his business and its current financial health; look into family, friends, community ties, whatever you can access to help you prepare for the visit. Don't waste time talking about your capital campaign with a foundation that has a policy against supporting capital projects—that's insulting to everyone involved.

A good development call is as much about hearing what the donor has to say as it is about presenting the case for your organization.

Part of the work of a qualifying call is to determine what will motivate the donor to become more involved in your organization. You want to get to know this person, to learn as much as possible about his interests, his volunteer activities, the kinds of projects he supports, what other nonprofit boards he sits on, his community involvement, and what gets him excited or passionate in his philanthropy. This type of conversation requires careful listening, as well as talking.

Back at the office, be sure that all qualifying calls have been recorded as a first step taken with that donor. Use either a major-gift-prospect tracking system or an excel spreadsheet to record the date, the participants, the key points, and the outcome of the meeting. Use your knowledge of the prospect to identify one or two next steps to take with that prospect. *Assign a date to each next step*. This will help you track and monitor your prospecting activity.

The goal of creating an individualized cultivation plan for a prospect is to develop a meaningful relationship between the prospect and your organization. You do this by beginning to integrate the prospect into the cultivation process you have already created. Examples of next steps might include:

- Invitation to a dinner, an event, or an opening that your group is planning

- Mailing of a campaign video, brochure, or commemorative item

- An invitation to become more involved in your organization as a volunteer, docent, speaker, or service provider

- A request that the person join a board or committee in your organization

The quality and sincerity of each interaction will help make the prospect a genuine fan and supporter of your organization even before you start talking about a gift. Don't skimp on personal touches, such as personal contacts by phone or e-mail, personal notes, and personal invitations to selected events. In these days of mass marketing, direct mail, and e-invite blasts, personal connections are worth more than ever before.

TIPS & TECHNIQUES

Sometimes, just getting in the door is the hardest part of a call. Here are a few tips that you can try.

How to Get an Appointment for a Qualifying Call:

- Ask a mutual friend, volunteer, or board member to open the door for you (they don't necessarily have to go along).

- Create a survey (e.g., on a topic related to your organization's work) and ask the prospect to be one of your survey participants.

- Include the prospect in a feasibility study or campaign planning study.

- Send an introductory letter about your organization and call to follow up on the letter.

- Make friends with the prospect's executive assistant.

- Describe one recent accomplishment briefly and use it to capture the prospect's attention.

- Set up a trip and tell the prospect you will be in his city only one day.

- Use the name of a peer (make sure you get permission first).

How to Ask for and Close the Gift

Components of the Solicitation Call

There are six main components to making a solicitation call, and they are all important to the success of the process. There is no substitute for experience when dealing with high-level donors. Passion, a just cause, and needs are all part of making a successful case, but professionalism, good training, and experience will always win the gift. If you are training new staff, a new executive director, or new board members in solicitation techniques, be sure to pair them with more experienced solicitors.

Preparation. Everyone will perform better and be more at ease if you plan out the call ahead of time. Assign roles, discuss how the group will handle objections, and set the ask amount. If necessary, bring everyone who will participate together face to face and run through a practice session. If a meeting isn't possible, hold a conference call to discuss the solicitation.

Consider writing out scripts, or at least bullet points, for key players. Show the team a sanitized summary of your prospect research (always keep confidentiality in mind), including the past giving total to the organization by this donor. Let your participants know that this call is important to you, to your organization, and to the campaign by staffing it well.

In some cases, the key decision is who should go on the call. The proper answer is: *whoever has the best chance of getting the gift.* Don't send more than three people on a call, or it will look like you are ganging up on the prospect. When planning a solicitation for a lead gift, select a team member from each of these groups: a board member or volunteer who knows the donor, the executive director or president, and the VP for advancement or another staff member who knows the donor.

Making the appointment sets the stage for the call. Consider doing it your-self, if you know the donor, or ask your volunteer who knows the prospect to set it up. A good executive secretary can also handle this job well, especially if she is already friendly with the donor or his staff. Request any equipment you will need, such as PowerPoint projectors, conference tables, screens, and VCR or DVD players, and let them know in advance who is coming.

Offer to meet on the donor's turf and let her choose the time and place based on her convenience. Restaurants and coffee shops are popular choices for meetings, but they lack privacy and the ambient noise can seriously hamper conversation. Try to find a place that is quiet where you won't be interrupted, such as a board room, office, home, or other private site.

Determine in advance if you would like to have the spouse present. In some cases, including the spouse can give you a strategic advantage. Don't make

 **LIVE & LEARN**

The leaders of a nonprofit were contacted by a prospect who had been indicted for business fraud but who wanted to make a large gift. The prospective donor claimed the indictment was politically moti-vated and assured them that the charges would be dismissed. The prospect made it clear that one of the reasons he wished to make the gift was to clear his name in the community.

While the nonprofit executives were interested in moving ahead with the gift, they decided to consult their board for advice. Board mem-bers called for caution, and they waited to close the gift until after the trial. When the would-be donor was convicted, discussions came to a screeching halt.

assumptions about who the decision maker is; women have become much more involved in philanthropic decision making over the past decade than ever before, and in many families the bulk of the assets may actually belong to the wife. Having the wife and husband present together can also bring the solicitation to a close earlier, because some married donors use the need to consult their spouse as a method of postponing a decision on making the gift.

Opening Gambits. There are always moments at the beginning of a call when people are getting settled, getting drinks, and introducing themselves. Assign one member of the solicitation team to take charge of your group; they should open with a short period of chit-chat, introduce everyone present, and make sure that the donor understands who everyone in the room is and their relationship within the organization.

The main purpose of the introduction period is to set everyone at ease, and it should last no more than five minutes. Have the person in charge make a smooth segue into the business at hand, and keep the conversation from getting awkward before moving into the case presentation.

Making the Case. The purpose of this segment of the call is to educate and to persuade, to convey to the donor through words, pictures, and feelings the importance of the project at hand. Making the case should be thought through ahead of time and assigned to one team member, preferably one who is very familiar with the organization and who can speak about its work with passion. This is a perfect role for the volunteer or board member, but it can also be an appropriate assignment for the executive director.

This segment of the call is where brochures, renderings, videos, PowerPoints, and other visual materials can be helpful to illustrate the need and the vision for the project under discussion. Depending on the duration of the entire call, and the level of knowledge that the donor already possesses about the organization, presenting the case should take about 20 minutes. Don't belabor it—it should be succinct, exciting, and focused on the future of the organization. Talking too long at this stage can be deadly to the ask.

Always relate the case back to the mission of your organization. Making the case involves answering several key questions:

- What is the mission of the organization?

- Where is the organization headed in the future?

- What are the needs that will be addressed in the future through this capital campaign?

- Why should this donor support this campaign?

- What is urgent about making this gift at this time?

Remember to use good interactive communication skills. Do more than talk at the prospect; while making the presentation, stop often to see if she has questions or comments, and keep her actively involved in the conversation.

Making the Ask. Assign making the ask to a team member other than the one selected to make the case. That way one person isn't doing all the talking, and a more natural flow can develop in the conversation. Have the team member who made the case turn to the person who will ask and prompt them with a lead-in, such as "Now Bob has something important to ask you."

A volunteer who is willing to ask and has made his own gift makes the best solicitor. A volunteer can say, "I've made my own gift of $100,000 to the campaign because it is very important to me, and now I'm asking you to do the same." This is a very powerful ask.

Be sure to clarify ahead of time that the volunteer is willing to mention, or have mentioned, the exact amount of his gift. Sometimes volunteers are more comfortable with putting themselves in a gift range, as in: "I want you to know that I have made a gift of seven figures to this campaign. That is how important this project is to me. I hope that we can count on you to make a gift of $1,000,000 also."

The executive director or the advancement team member can also be excellent solicitors, especially if someone else on the team has made the case presentation earlier. The focus of the meeting then moves from one person saying, "This is the project at hand, and I am passionate about it for these reasons," to "This project can't be completed without your help. We'd like you to help us make it happen. Do you think you could support us with a gift of $100,000?"

It is very important to ask for a specific amount. An ask hasn't been completed unless a dollar figure is put forward by the person asking. It is a common weakness for a solicitor to stop short of articulating a specific number and lead with a vague statement such as: "Do you think you can help us out?" There may be a few unique circumstances where this approach is successful, but 90% of the time, this approach will kill or lower your gift. *The biggest reason for solicitation failures is a failure to actually ask for the money.*

It has become a development truism that after you make the ask, you should stay silent until the prospective donor responds. This is also a negotiating tactic used in business dealings; put out your first offer, then sit tight and see what the counteroffer looks like. Silence makes people sitting together very uncomfortable, but you need to endure it. Speaking first will weaken your ability to negotiate and to settle possible differences that may arise in the ensuing discussion.

Listen and Assess the Donor's Response. There are many possible objections that can arise at this point in a solicitation call, and a whole host of avenues to pursue to keep gift options open. The key here is to remain flexible, listen carefully, and not overreach what you promise the donor.

Take each objection at face value, and try to answer it calmly and firmly. No matter what objections are raised, always come back to focus on the gift: "What can we do, Mr. and Mrs. Smith, to help bring you to a decision on making this gift?"

Try to agree on next steps that will benefit both sides. You may decide together that the donors need to make a visit to your site to see your programs; you might ask for permission to consult with their financial adviser; you may need to supply specific answers to questions they raise. Whatever the objection is, try to keep the ask open and the attitude positive.

Should the conversation move in a negative direction, consider asking for more time or for a hearing on different terms. Instead of leaving with a definite *no*, say, "I understand that your stock is down a little right now. Could we come back and talk to you in six months?" One donor recently countered after an ask was made that his adult children were now active on his foundation board and their interests were in different areas. In response, the group asked to make the same presentation in front of the children to help them understand the needs of the organization. The donor was delighted and helped to set up the meeting.

This point in the discussion is also a good time to bring up planned giving options. Comments from the prospect about a pending retirement, supporting a child, or estate issues should be your cue to say that perhaps there is a planned giving alternative that would meet their needs and still allow them to make a gift to your campaign. Advanced training and expertise need to come into play here, but all major gifts officers and executive directors should be trained in basic planned giving techniques (see Chapter 8).

Do not automatically offer a pledge payout period during the solicitation phase of the call. Hold back on the pledge as an option to use in your response to the donor's objections. For instance, if you ask for $100,000, and the prospect responds, "I can only do $25,000 at this time," follow up with a request that they consider $25,000 a year for four years. You still get the gift, and they meet their cash-flow needs.

Closing the Gift. For some people the most difficult part of the solicitation is closing the gift. Some donors leave the conversation open for years and let the gift discussion drift while they put you off; others will quickly move to offer a much smaller gift than the one you asked for in order to get rid of you. Your role is stay focused on getting a *specific dollar amount and timetable agreed to in writing*. The next best choice is to leave with a specific plan of action. Do not leave the meeting with only a vague promise that "you'll hear from me soon."

After the call, spend a minute debriefing and don't forget to write a thank-you note to everyone involved. Track the meeting in your prospect-tracking system and enter the next steps into the prospect's record. The average ratio of gifts made per donor solicited is one out of three or four, so don't feel badly if not all your calls are successful.

TIPS & TECHNIQUES

Here Are Some Helpful Suggestions for Closing the Meeting:

- May I call you next week to see if you've had time to discuss this further with your family?

- I'd like to help you put your expectations into a pledge letter. Should I send a draft to your office?

- Do you think I could send some sample bequest language to your attorney?

- When would be a good day for you to come down and tour the site?

- Do you think we could revise this proposal and get together again next week to talk about your concerns?

- I understand that you might not be able to make a gift of that size now, but would you consider pledging it over several years?

- We will have some new architectural plans ready next month. Could I come back and show them to you and your wife then? I think they will address some of your concerns.

The Prospect Who Didn't Close the Door

A nonprofit made a leadership gift call for their capital campaign on a prominent businessman who had supported them in the past with small annual gifts. The prospect had never made a major gift, but he certainly had the capacity to do so. He was asked to make the lead gift to name their new facility for $2.5 million.

The call was a difficult one; the donor challenged some of the directions the executive director laid out and asked tough questions about how they were using money they already had. The team tried their best, but they left feeling discouraged.

Over the next 18 months, the three members of the team that made the call took turns keeping in touch with him. They made contact at least once a month, sent him materials, invited him to events, or called with updates on the project. He did visit the site of the new facility, but he never said yes or no to making the gift.

Finally, the campaign chair called and asked to sit down with him again. Much to the chair's surprise, the donor agreed to the gift. He explained that the long delay was due to his having sold his business and made plans for his estate. The gift ended up being a combination of income from a trust and cash that served the needs of both parties.

Moral of the story: Don't give up too soon. Persistence and patience are useful virtues in development.

CHAPTER 7

Strategies That Motivate Donors

 After reading this chapter, you will be able to:

- Use naming recognition and challenges to motivate donors.
- Raise sights with donors to increase gift levels.
- Plan effective stewardship and donor recognition.

Naming Opportunities and Challenge Gifts

Your goal with donors in the capital campaign is not only to motivate them to become committed to the campaign and to make a gift, but to make a gift that will make a difference. Encouraging a donor to give to his capacity, as opposed to making a smaller commitment or a token gift, is a complex process that involves many variables. Not all of these variables can be influenced by the fundraiser; for instance, you cannot control the vagaries of the stock market on the donor's portfolio. You can separate variables, however, and concentrate on those you do have some control over. One important motivating tool that you can control in a capital campaign is the offer of donor recognition through naming opportunities.

Pricing Naming Opportunities

In campaigns that involve a building project, or a capital renovation, the advancement team needs to be involved with the architect and building planners from the beginning of the project to identify and price naming options. Most capital campaign planners prepare a list of naming opportunities for donor recognition, with prices attached, before the campaign solicitations begin. This list becomes a key element of the solicitation and ensuing negotiation.

In some cases, the project won't have reached the point where the planning required to create the recognition list is completed, but it is still necessary for the organization to start raising money to produce cash flow. You can go ahead and start solicitations, using the site plans and renderings that are available, but be cautious about promises made to donors. In such cases, it is important to reassure donors that they will have an early option on naming recognition when plans are complete. Be sure that donors know at least the basics of the recognition options surrounding their gift level, for instance, whether it will name an internal or external component of the project.

How should you price your naming options? First, start with your overall campaign goal. If you need to raise $10 million for a building, your list of naming opportunities should add up to at least $10 million. Many professionals recommend making the list total at least 20 to 30% more than the total funds you require; this allows some cushion in case you can't sell all the recognition opportunities, prices go up, or pledges go unpaid. (With construction project costs on the rise, prices almost always go up from initial estimates, and you might as well plan for the needs you are going to encounter.) For a $10 million campaign, this would mean setting the total sum of naming options at $12 million or $13 million.

Separate out your external naming recognition from internal options. In general, you can command a premium for external naming recognition. Be tasteful, and be careful not to go overboard on naming overlapping external entities. It can be confusing to donors and visitors to your new building to find the Smith Wing of the Johnson Building in the Jones Pavilion on the Baker Campus. Some states have legal requirements that affect naming rights; for instance, in Louisiana, it is not legal to name a building owned by the State after a living donor (this was imposed to halt graft and corruption). Make sure you are familiar with any local, state, or federal regulations that might affect your project.

When determining the price for the external naming of a building, consider these three factors: the total cost of the project; the market price in your region for external naming; and the capacity of the prospects at the top of your gift table. Many campaign consultants recommend setting the external naming price at 30% to 50% of the total project cost. In other words, if the project total is $10 million, the external name would be priced from $3 million to $5 million.

However, there are significant regional differences in ability to command naming prices, and this should be factored into your planning. Do some local market research; canvas your community, and become familiar with the local university, hospital, museum, and school pricing levels. If you are located in a small town without a significant corporate base, $3 million may be perceived as a prohibitive amount for naming your $10 million building. If your organization is conducting a national campaign, or if you are located in the more affluent northeastern or western coasts, $5 million may seem very attractive to a potential donor to name a $10 million project.

Also make sure that you have a prospective donor who can afford your naming price! While you don't want to undersell your opportunities, you must be realistic, or your campaign will end up in trouble. If your organization's top gift to date has been $500,000 and your top prospect is rated at $1 million, then pricing your building's name at $3 million is a risky strategy. Should you do it anyway, in the hopes that the campaign could attract a gift of that size? Maybe, but make a backup plan for what you will do if the gift fails to materialize.

Once you have set the external naming price, which will determine how much you have left to raise to meet your goal, start listing the internal options available to you. Divide up the remaining funds that you will need to raise and start allocating costs by floor, room, and use of each space. Do not try to match each component with the actual cost of that piece of the project, a mistake often made by operations and construction management overseers who are trained to view the project on a literal cost-per-square-footage basis. Recognition is about prominence, visibility, and overall attractiveness of the space, not size and cost.

For example, in a sample campaign with a $10 million goal for a capital project, the prices might look something like Exhibit 7.1. Naming rights for the first floor are set at $500,000 more than the second floor, due to the enhanced traffic and visibility of the first floor, and the larger meeting rooms and entrance lobby are priced at levels above the less visible spaces. Internal and external functional elements, such as exhibits, major pieces of equipment, landscaping, and furnishings can also be a part of your pricing structure. Note that the total list adds up to $12 million, more than the stated goal, to cover for extra expenses and unsold areas.

Some capital campaigns have started adding a surcharge, or "tax," on top of naming opportunities to cover current or future operating expenses, such as paying for capital campaign fundraising, or creating a maintenance fund to keep up the buildings once they have been completed. While this may be sound financial reasoning, you probably will want to test this concept with your early donors. You don't want to lose donors over these assessments. Make sure that you are honest and direct about any hidden costs you are applying against capital gifts, or you could have angry donors on your hands.

EXHIBIT 7.1

Capital Campaign for a
$10,000,000 Classroom Building

Recognition Opportunities and Prices

External Name of the Building	$ 5,000,000
First Floor	$ 1,500,000
Second Floor	$ 1,000,000
Entrance Lobby	$ 750,000
Auditorium	$ 750,000
Exterior Courtyard	$ 500,000
Dean's Suite	$ 500,000
Conference Suite	$ 500,000
Classrooms (5 @ $100,000 each)	$ 500,000
Faculty Offices (5 @ $50,000 each)	$ 250,000
Interior Courtyard	$ 250,000
Computer Labs (4 @ $50,000 each)	$ 200,000
Student Lounge	$ 150,000
Faculty Lounge	$ 150,000
Total of Named Spaces	**$ 12,000,000**

The Courtyard That Kept Disappearing

In a capital campaign for a new science building wing, one university architect created a preliminary plan that included an attractive external courtyard. The advancement team offered the courtyard-naming rights to the first donor to the campaign, a prominent businessman, for $500,000.

Later plans deleted the courtyard, which became a victim of "value engineering," or cost cutting, applied to the project to meet bottom-line budget goals. Although the advancement staff complained, the courtyard was taken out and put back in three times during the planning process.

With good communication developed between the advancement staff and the project's architect, a less costly version of the courtyard concept was finally implemented. At the dedication, lovely plantings and landscaping distinguished the space. The donor was happy and the pledge was paid.

Matches and Challenges

Challenge matches, which have been used for years in annual fund campaigns, also are being effectively used in capital campaign settings. Timing, the amount of the challenge, and how the challenge is used by the advancement team are all important components of making the strategy work for your organization. Don't hesitate to approach a donor with one of the ideas outlined below; you don't have to wait for a challenge to appear, you can make it happen. Many donors are thrilled to have a nonprofit use their gifts to publicly encourage others to give. Challenge matches make great publicity, create results, and can build campaign momentum and spirit.

Some matches or challenges work best at the beginning of the campaign, in the quiet phase, and apply only to lead donors, board members, and other insiders. A board member, for instance, could challenge the other members of the board to reach a "Leadership Fund" goal of $1,000,000, and the challenging board member gives the first $100,000. This kind of early competition can be a good way to motivate those who are close to the organization to pledge their gifts at a time when their support is critical to setting the pace for others who will follow.

Another option is to use a challenge later in the public part of the campaign, perhaps when a lull or pause in major gift giving occurs. A leadership donor who gave early in the campaign could be approached to make a second gift, for example, and to challenge other early donors to do the same. One tactic along these lines is to challenge donors who gave in the quiet phase to add an additional year to the term of their pledge payments; for a campaign that has accepted mostly five-year pledges, this would effectively raise the giving totals by 20% overall.

Many advancement professionals prefer using a challenge or match in the final stages of the public phase of the campaign as a technique for motivating smaller donors, or those who are not as close to the organization, to make a gift. Challenges and matches can be used to attract gifts from members of new constituencies, for instance, building a base among those who may not have formerly supported your efforts. You may want to structure the match so that all gifts from new donors up to a certain goal are matched 2:1 by a gift from a generous donor, for instance.

Some foundations, such as the Kresge Foundation, which supports capital campaigns across the nation, prefer to have their commitments used to challenge new donors during the final stages of a campaign. The concept of building a base of new donors who could be tapped for future support is very attractive to funding groups whose goal is to make nonprofits more accountable and self-sustaining. Be sure you have the planning and infrastructure available to make the challenge work, however, or you may end up being embarrassed when you have to tell a major supporter that their challenge hasn't been met.

Sight-Raising Techniques

Sight-raising is the fundraising term that refers to motivating donors to make larger gifts. There are many ways to encourage donors to maximize their giving potential, but you must begin with a donor who has the giving capacity to make a larger gift. All the techniques in the world won't help to move a donor from $1,000 to $10,000 if he really doesn't have the financial means to make the larger gift. Sight-raising is about creating an environment in which the norm, or the expectation, is that donors will give to a certain new level, and that new level is higher than their former level.

LIVE & LEARN

A donor made an extremely generous gift to name the imposing entrance lobby of a new hospital facility. The hospital offered to hang a portrait of the philanthropist and his wife in the lobby, which the donor readily agreed to. The hospital chose one of the leading portrait artists in town, and, after numerous sittings, the portrait was unveiled at the building's dedication. Unfortunately the donor hated the painting and insisted that it be taken down immediately.

Subsequently the donor demanded a new portrait and chose his own artist. The painting was completed, paid for by the hospital (for the second time), and hung in the entrance lobby. The old one remains in the attic, to gather dust for future generations.

Setting a Higher Standard for Gifts

Most donors will give to you because they support your cause. How you state your case, the urgency of your mission, and the perceived need for your services are all important reasons why your donors give to you. However, there are other, more subtle, factors that come into play when someone decides *how large a gift* to make to your campaign.

Many donors respond to cues that they receive from their peers, the recognition they are offered, and their understanding of what other donors are giving. This happens because many leadership donors are active in their social or business milieu; they care about how their gifts are perceived by their peers, and they have competitive instincts that play a role in their philanthropic decisions.

From the very beginning of your campaign, you are giving out signals to your capital campaign committee members, board members, and early donors about the gift levels you expect from them. These signals include the total size of your campaign, the giving levels on your gift table, the prices assigned to major recognition opportunities, and the level of early gifts from your leaders.

Plan to share your gift table and the recognition opportunities list with prices with all your leadership groups before solicitations begin. If the campaign gift table requires the majority of gifts to come in at $25,000 or more, and the board and leadership is committed to making the campaign succeed, then *they need to see themselves* as giving gifts of $25,000 or more.

Early gifts from board and campaign leaders are absolutely critical in setting the bar for those that follow. If your first three gifts, from your campaign chair, your board chair, and your closest donor, are each at the $1,000,000 level, they transmit a very powerful, but unstated, message: *Gifts of $1,000,000 and more are expected if you want to be a leader in this campaign.*

In order to produce this result, you must carefully strategize with your campaign leadership about which gifts are solicited and announced first, as well as what their own commitments will be.

It is common for leadership gifts to cluster within a certain dollar range. In one campaign, it may be at the $250,000 level, but in another, *given donors of the same capacity,* it may only be at the $25,000 level. What makes the difference? It is often a combination of peer pressure, early gift levels, the perceived status of the organization within the community, and the donor's perception of the value of the recognition offered.

The total campaign goal can also be a factor in gift size because some donors think of their gift as a percentage of the total goal. For instance, a donor might give $1,000,000 as a leadership gift in a $10,000,000 campaign (10% of the total), while *the same donor* would only give $100,000 in a $1,000,000 campaign (this gift is also 10% of the total).

This illustrates a conclusion that may seem counterintuitive, but often holds true: donors will often make larger gifts in a bigger campaign, all other factors being equal. This is one reason why campaigns sometimes set a "reach" goal, or a goal higher than what the organization might normally think it could raise.

Framing the Ask

Another technique for sight-raising with donors takes place during the actual solicitation process. If a donor has been properly cultivated, she will already be relatively familiar with your case and your campaign needs before the solicitation call. Often, by simply accepting the solicitation appointment, the donor is signaling that she intends to make a gift. But how big a gift? While many

RULES OF THE ROAD

The Edifice Complex: the urge that men of a certain age get to put their name on a building.

donors will have a number in mind before the solicitation call, how you and your solicitors "frame" the ask amount can influence the total gift pledged.

Prepare carefully the materials you will use to show the prospective donor. If you plan to make an ask of $100,000, for instance, prepare a list of all your other donors who have already made gifts from $50,000 to $250,000. Use their names, if they have given you permission to do so. When you make the solicitation, ask the donor for $100,000 and show her the list. Let her see who has already committed at that level.

Including donors one level up and one level down from the solicitation level helps her to see her gift in context. She knows she isn't the largest donor, but she isn't the smallest one either. She will probably also recognize names of other donors whom she knows, which will help her make a commitment.

Another technique for adding context to a solicitation is to use your campaign gift table as a handout in the solicitation. Prepare the gift table so that it illustrates not only how many gifts are needed at each level, but how many have been pledged at each level. As you make the ask for a specific amount, point out to the donor where that gift level lies on the gift table; this allows him to see his gift in relation to others needed and given in the levels above and below his potential gift.

TIPS & TECHNIQUES

Naming opportunity and recognition lists can be prepared for calls by cutting off lower levels to guide the donor to certain gift amounts. If you are asking for $100,000, don't emphasize gift recognition options at $25,000 and $50,000.

Create a version called "Leadership Gift Recognition" and let it reflect recognition levels of $100,000 and up, or write a proposal that suggests two or three options at $100,000 and leave the rest of the list at home.

Using Communication Tools Effectively

There are some communication and PR techniques regarding your campaign that can help you with sight-raising. At board meetings, for instance, only announce individual gifts above a certain level; select a level that is commensurate with the standard you and your leaders have set for board gifts. In other words, if the leadership gift level in your campaign is $100,000, then announce gifts of $100,000 and more *by name* when you report on the campaign totals in front of your board.

You can also follow the same technique when communicating with your external audiences. Use your local newspaper, campaign newsletter, and Web site to carry announcements of gifts, with donors' names, at your leadership gift level. Make sure you have the donor's permission to use their name before any announcement, public or in-house, is made, and ask the donor how he wants his name to appear. (It is a good idea to get this information signed off on in a pledge document at the time the gift is made.)

The campaign newsletter and Web site present special opportunities to focus on gifts of a certain size. Carefully structure and time your stories about donors and gifts to focus on your needs; for instance, if you are about to start phase one of the construction project, interview your lead donor to phase one about why he made his gift. In another issue, focus on planned giving, and ask one of your bequest donors to allow you to feature her gift.

Personal stories and examples of philanthropy from donors of lead gifts will help to make all of your constituents aware that large gifts are not only likely, they are actually occurring. Perhaps there is some basic group psychology at work here; if a donor sees that your campaign is getting gifts of $1,000,000, it becomes easier for him to see himself giving a gift of $1,000,000.

Donor Recognition and Stewardship

Advancement professionals often harp on good stewardship, the treatment of donors after a gift is made. Sometimes, however, stewardship is the last thing on the minds of harried campaign staff members, who are pushed to bring in more new gifts.

Why is stewardship so important? Donors who are treated well are more willing to become donors again. Donors who are already familiar with your organization require less staff and volunteer time to research, cultivate, and solicit than do new donors. It just makes good economic sense to build strong relationships with donors who are with you now.

Planning a Donor Recognition Continuum

Donor recognition needs to be thought through from the commencement of the capital campaign. Think about the needs of all donors, from the very top to the bottom of your gift table. Many campaigns do a pretty good job with the big donors, those who name buildings or create endowments, but they lose their focus as the gift sizes go down. Smaller donors are important; they build the base for your future campaigns, they talk to others in their community about your organization, and they may become big donors someday. So treat them right!

Recognition through the use of named spaces has been covered above, but what about plaques, lists, Web sites, publications, bricks, and donor walls? It is smart to set your rules early for how you will recognize gifts at all levels, and educate your staff, volunteers, and donors so that everyone is clear about your policies. This is a good area in which to get advice from your campaign committee members (see Exhibit 7.2). You can be sure they will have opinions.

Here are some organizing principles to consider in donor recognition:

- Recognize gifts according to purpose. For instance, don't mix recognition of gifts for annual operations with capital gifts.
- Determine what levels of gifts will be recognized.
- Determine how and where each level of gift will be recognized.

- Determine how (and if) you will recognize gifts that are revocable, such as bequests and unrealized planned gifts from trusts or life insurance.

- Create a policy for the use of signage, plaques, and naming recognition throughout the capital project and stick to your plan.

EXHIBIT 7.2

Sample Donor Recognition Continuum

Under $100	Listed in the annual report in the year they made a gift
$100–$499	Join lowest-level donor club
	Listed on the Web site for the duration of the campaign
	Listed in the annual report in the year they made gift
	Sent a certificate thanking them for their gift
$500–$999	All of the above, but they go into a higher-level donor club for the annual report and Web site
$1,000–$9,999	Listed on a permanent donor wall in the new facility
	Listed on Web site and in annual report in next level of donor club
	Listed in the final campaign report that announces the end of the campaign and thanks donors
$10,000–$500,000	Given naming recognition with custom signage inside the new facility

---

EXHIBIT 7.2 (CONTINUED)

	Listed on permanent donor wall in next level of donor club
	Listed in campaign report
	Invited to dedication ceremony for new facility
$1,000,000+	Given external naming recognition with custom signage on the outside of the new facility
	Article written about the gift for local newspaper
	Special dedication ceremony to honor the donor
	Listed on permanent donor wall in biggest typeface
	Gift featured in campaign report

Special Issues in Donor Recognition

Donor societies are a useful and familiar way to honor donors at different levels. If your organization wishes to be democratic and list donors of all levels without singling out gift size, consider publishing the groups of names without dollar amounts, using the print size to distinguish smaller donors from larger ones. Donor societies can be useful in moving donors up to new levels of giving in capital campaigns, just as they are used in annual campaigns.

Lifetime giving societies are a special leadership donor society for lifetime donors of a total amount, as opposed to recognition for one-time or annual gifts. The lifetime giving society allows you to set a very high accumulated gift level—such as $500,000 or $1,000,000—and honor those special families or donors who have truly made a difference over the long-term for your organization.

Having such a lifetime donor society also gives you another good tool to use in raising sights with donors to the capital campaign who are nearing the gift total for joining the group. Make the induction ceremony into the group something very special, post pictures of the new members on your Web site, and your donors will be eager to join.

Special events or donor benefits can be attached to gifts of different levels, and may be especially useful in campaigns where your donors like to mix and mingle with each other. Universities, where alumni have common ties, or health-related causes, where donors share special concerns, often use events tied to giving levels as a way to promote group camaraderie.

A donor, for instance, may be motivated to give $1,000 to the capital campaign in order to receive an invitation to the annual ball for the Founders Circle. Remember that IRS regulations require you to inform donors of the market value of any benefits they may receive. Give your donors the chance to opt out if they want to get a full tax write-off.

Corporate donors are often interested in sponsorships and naming rights that have publicity value for their businesses. The rules of corporate giving are changing rapidly, and they are moving more toward a contractual relationship paid for with marketing dollars rather than making a philanthropic contribution to a nonprofit. You may decide to roll with the times, but be sure that you are ready for the challenge; you will need to know the details of your media market, be able to guarantee the number of visitors who will see the corporate logo in your new building, and be prepared to co-brand your institution to support a company's image in the marketplace.

Frequently, the terms of recognition for corporate gifts are different from the terms for foundations or individuals. Consider limiting the contractual naming obligation for a corporate gift to a capital project to a defined number of years; this allows you to go back to the original donor in year 5 or year 10 to ask for a new gift, or to resell the recognition opportunity to a different donor down the line.

There can be a downside for nonprofits in accepting a corporate marketing connection without some advance consideration. For some organizations, a

TIPS & TECHNIQUES

Beware the Enron effect. It may be wise to vet the issue of corporate sponsorships and naming rights thoroughly with your board before entering a campaign. Examine the needs and desires of your institution in light of your history, your mission, and community norms before committing to a gift that might undermine the image you have carefully built for your nonprofit.

Be picky—if you are the executive director of your region's largest conservation organization, you might not want to be paired on the six o'clock news with the state's largest polluter. Don't forget that most businesses are interested in partnering with you to enhance their name, not necessarily to promote yours.

corporate partnership may feel like "selling out." For others, corporate-sponsored advertising may be the best method of attracting public attention and perfectly appropriate.

Recognition for Bequests and other Planned Gifts can be a tricky matter in campaigns. First of all, separate recognition issues from counting issues; they are related, but not the same. You may wish to count bequests or other revocable gifts on a separate line in your campaign totals, but this doesn't mean that you should be putting a bequest expectancy donor's name on a room in your new building.

In deference to donors who are actually giving you cash and paying on pledges, it is not standard practice to give naming recognition for a planned gift that has not yet been realized. (Once the planned gift is received, of course, you should honor the donor in an appropriate manner.) There are always exceptions to every rule, however, and you don't want to lose a large bequest over recognition issues. If a donor is determined on receiving naming rights for a bequest or other planned gift, try to work with him and his advisers to make the gift irrevocable. Putting the gift into an irrevocable trust, for instance, might be an acceptable option for both sides.

The dilemma arises in how to make a planned giving donor feel special while he is still alive and well to enjoy the attention, but your organization hasn't yet received the gift. Often the planned giving donor feels that he has made a gift, sometimes a very large one, and he expects special treatment. The most common answer to this problem is to create a planned giving donor society.

The planned giving donor society allows you to honor all donors who have named your organization in their wills without being intrusive about amounts, terms, and other personal estate-planning details. Planned giving donor society members can be invited to special functions, their names can be listed on donor walls and in publications, and they can be given a special commemorative item. It is simply good stewardship to keep up with these donors, because they can change the terms of their will or bequest if they choose to do so.

Planned giving donors are often willing to be featured in ads, stories, and brochures about making planned gifts to your organization. Because their stories often have emotional impact, they can influence others who are thinking about making planned gifts. This is an effective way to increase recognition for the donor and to increase the awareness among your donor base about planned gift alternatives.

Stewardship toward the Next Gift

Good stewardship is the key to bringing donors back to make additional gifts. Whether it is for annual giving, capital campaign gifts, or planned gifts, donors want to be kept informed, be treated right, and have their intentions honored. Many major gift experts now talk about building "lifetime relationships" with donors, from the first gift to the bequest, and appropriate stewardship is the basic currency of this relationship.

TIPS & TECHNIQUES

An endowment gift can be the cornerstone for a larger planned gift. A viable option for giving recognition for a planned gift is to ask the donor to create a named, endowed fund while he is still alive with a smaller cash gift. Work with the donor so that when the planned gift matures, the funds can be added to the endowed fund that already exists. Family members can also contribute to help the endowed fund grow.

This technique allows the donor to make a meaningful contribution to your organization's future (through the planned gift), but it also gives the donor the advantage of seeing the fund created during his lifetime (with the smaller cash gift). With appropriate stewardship, the donor will receive recognition and see some benefit from the fund's creation and activity while he is alive to enjoy it.

What are the components of good stewardship? Most campaign stewardship starts with the receipt of the gift and continues until the next gift is made. Sometimes, for leadership gifts that are critically important to the campaign, an individual stewardship plan is created for the leadership donor.

Basic Components of a Stewardship Plan:

- Send out a receipt right away with the correct information.

- Send personal thank-yous; these might be letters or calls from the executive director, the VP for advancement, and the campaign chair.

- Confirm with the donor, in writing, the basic terms of the gift: the naming rights being offered, the full gift amount, the pledge period with dates, how the donor wants his name listed (or not listed), and the purpose of the gift.

- Keep the terms of the gift on file so that if there are staffing changes the gift will still be handled correctly.

- Adhere to the terms of the gift!

- Keep the donor informed about the use of the gift.

- For donors of endowed gifts, supply annual reports on the endowment's growth, payout, and use.

- Create personalized annual stewardship reports: for gifts over a certain size, say $1,000,000 for a large organization or $100,000 for a smaller one, create individualized reports once a year to update donors on

IN THE REAL WORLD

When a Gift Goes Bad

The basic goal of stewardship is to keep the donor tied to the organization by communicating on a regular, positive basis about the good results the gift has produced. The converse is also true; if problems arise regarding a gift, such as a major delay in construction, or problems with a program that require you to stop providing services, it is wise to own up to the problem.

One university had a large gift for an endowed chair that proved difficult to fill. The donor was never notified about the problem and the funds from the endowment were used to support other faculty members. The donor finally learned what was happening and threatened to sue (it is illegal to use the income from an endowment for purposes other than those specified by the donor). It took many meetings to calm him down and his goodwill was forever lost.

This could have been amicably resolved with earlier and better communication. Let the donor know *when the problem arises* what the issues are and how you propose to solve them. Ask for a change in the purpose of the gift as a last resort. Letting such problems fester can lay the foundation for hurt feelings, public denunciations, and lawsuits.

the status of their gift. Be creative; these reports might include thank-yous from students receiving a scholarship, a letter from the beneficiary of services provided through the donor's gift, or pictures of the new facility.

Summary

There are a variety of strategies and techniques that can help an organization motivate and build positive relationships with donors. From the development of naming options and recognition plans to the stewardship of gifts that have been received, you can help create a giving environment where your donors feel appreciated, involved, and part of the mission of your organization. The end result of good donor recognition and stewardship programs is a donor who is motivated to make her best gift to your campaign, to stay connected to the organization beyond the campaign, and to give again as a result of her lifetime relationship with you.

CHAPTER 8

Repositioning Your Organization through the Capital Campaign

After reading this chapter, you will be able to:

- Reach out to new constituencies.
- Use planned giving tools in the campaign.
- Coordinate your annual fund with your campaign.
- Plan for future needs.

Meeting Longer Term Goals of the Campaign

Capital campaigns are defined by their short-term goals: they are confined to specific projects, they have set time limits, and they focus on raising larger gifts restricted to the purpose and goals of the campaign. The organization as a whole benefits from the capital campaign to the extent that those purposes are met, as the nonprofit finishes the campaign with a new building, a bigger endowment, or an enhanced program.

With some foresight and planning, however, you can also use your campaign to meet some longer-term goals: reach out to new constituencies; build a larger and broader base of donors; and improve the professionalism, skills, and depth of your advancement program. Your organization can emerge from the campaign stronger, more flexible, and better positioned for the future.

Reaching Out to New Constituencies

Women, Minorities, and First-Time Donors in the Campaign

In the past few decades in the United States, a significant shift has occurred in wealth management, as economic and financial clout has passed to individuals and groups that traditionally have not been in charge of large amounts of assets. In some cases, this shift took place because members of diverse groups are playing a larger role in the nation's economy and earning more; the recent wealth of some Native American groups through the casino industry is one example of this trend.

In other cases, wealth distribution has shifted because women have a greater say in the use of disposable income from their households. Even more important for its fundraising implications, the majority of women in the United States now outlive their spouses, which often leaves them with assets and income that they can use for purposes of their own choosing.

While historically all Americans have found significant ways to be active in philanthropy, many members of minority groups have focused their giving on institutions and churches in their own communities. Today, people with access to wealth, no matter what their background or origins, have begun to assert themselves in ways that were formerly defined by the great philanthropists of the last century, men like the Rockefellers, Carnegies, or Fords. They are naming buildings, creating endowments, and taking on the leadership role in capital campaigns. There may be ways that your organization can do more to provide support for donors who are trying on new roles as philanthropists.

Perhaps the most important way that an organization can tap the giving power of new donor groups is to provide them with a voice and a vote on the organization's board. Not all prospects who have the financial potential to be leadership donors will want to be on your board, but some will. Many major donors see their gift as one part of a larger relationship with the organization, a relationship that can be strengthened by involvement with the nonprofit's programs and governance.

Volunteer involvement, of course, is not limited to board appointments. Many donors whose primary philanthropic experience has been with churches and grassroots social organizations wish to become involved in a real way with advancing the mission of your nonprofit. Their involvement will reap benefits on the giving side also. This may mean expanding the role of volunteers in your organization beyond planning the next auction or fundraising event.

While many nonprofits excel at providing meaningful volunteer experiences, others seem reluctant to include volunteers in the core activities that are central to their mission. In some cases, experience and credentials may play a role in these decisions; a volunteer cannot take the place of a university faculty member with a PhD in Art History. On the other hand, trained volunteers can offer job counseling advice and internships to college students, and the experience of mentoring a young person may be the tie that cements a bond between the volunteer and her alma mater.

The capital campaign offers special opportunities for broader interaction with diverse communities. If giving is related to involvement, then giving from diverse communities equates with involving those communities in the life of the organization. The symphony, for example, can develop a fund to add prominent minority guest artists to its programming, and begin to feature performances

LIVE & LEARN

The prominent and successful business owner wanted to give back to the university he graduated from. He arranged to name a new wing of the business school with a gift of several million dollars. In preparation for the dedication of the new facility, he was asked for his guest list. After naming several family members, he asked the advancement office to look up any of his old professors who were still alive and invite them to the dedication ceremony.

The advancement staff took on the task with enthusiasm, locating many emeritus professors living in retirement and inviting them to the dedication. Many of them responded positively and did attend. The donor, who was thrilled with the ceremony, remarked afterwards: "I was so glad to see my old professors there. They were the ones who gave me all those Cs and Ds, and now they all know how well I did."

beyond the traditional classical repertoire. The university can make the effort to involve minority alumni in the life of the institution in meaningful ways, such as raising scholarship funds for new minority students. Tying these outreach efforts to new facilities or to endowments can bring new groups into capital campaign fundraising.

An additional consideration in working with first-time donors is the issue of appropriate recognition. Some donors are not interested in seeing their name in lights on the outside of a major new building, and actually shy away from the naming rights that accrue to major gifts in a capital campaign. Sometimes those brought up in the more conservative pre–World War II era view it as unseemly to display their giving in a public manner. Other donors are more interested in the effect that their gift has on the organization than in the personal recognition that accrues through making the gift. Whatever the reason, it is important to be aware of differences in attitude toward recognition in working with first-time donors.

Approaching first-time donors for major capital gifts doesn't require different skills or strategies, but it may take a period of time to build the trust and commitment required for the donor to make a leadership gift. Many first-time donors are experiencing their first generation of wealth, with the attitudes and experiences that recently acquired wealth brings. For instance, entrepreneurs may be experts at wealth acquisition, but not know much about the tax advantages of making a gift. Experienced solicitors will focus on donor education and take extra time to build the relationships and personal trust that these donors require before a leadership gift can be realized.

 IN THE REAL WORLD

It's All Relative

One university president visited the widow of a wealthy board member who had been involved in the institution for most of his life. "We would love to have a building on our campus named for your husband," the president said. "He was instrumental to our success over the past decade. We would like to ask you to honor him with a gift that would allow us to recognize his name for future generations to come."

"I would like that too," said the widow. "But I'm sorry, I just can't; I'm very worried about the future. You see, I'm down to my last $20 million."

To approach a first-time donor for the capital campaign, emphasize good basic fundraising tactics:

- *Treat him as if he were a major donor already.* Use the same level of volunteer that you would use with donors who are better known to you. A prospective new donor will be pleased if he is approached by a corporate leader, your CEO, or a board member.

- *Explain in clear business terms what the goals of the campaign are.* Most first-time major donors made their own money. They are smart in business and know how to leverage a dollar.

- *Focus on outcomes.* Make it clear why an investment in your project would be a good investment for them and for the community.

- *Be persistent.* Sometimes an individual new to giving isn't ready to make a commitment to philanthropy at his first exposure to the concept.

- *Involve both spouses in the solicitation.* Your goal is to educate the prospective donor couple about how to use their money to bring a project to fruition and to help them play a larger role in their community.

- *Add a social dimension.* Many first-time donors are new to the social aspects of nonprofit donor circles. Invite the couple to a private dinner, a small party, or a benefit event. This makes them feel a part of your organization's inner circle. Your job is to make sure they feel welcome!

- *Practice good stewardship.* Make the donor feel good about giving. You are helping to create a philanthropist who will probably give back to more than just your organization, and who can pass on the thrill of giving to his children and grandchildren.

Fundraising Tools

The capital campaign gives your advancement team the opportunity to add depth and experience. While major gifts may be the lifeblood of the capital campaign fundraising effort, planned giving tools can be helpful in closing campaign gifts. Most organizations also have to continue some form of annual giving during a campaign, which requires careful coordination to avoid annoying prospects with conflicting solicitations. Finally, it is useful to be aware of some trends in nonprofit fundraising that could influence your planning efforts.

Planned Giving in the Capital Campaign

If your staff and volunteers are trained in planned giving techniques, planned gifts can play an important role in your campaign. Sometimes nonprofit leaders are biased against planned gifts because they know they won't get the cash right away; however, this attitude represents short-term thinking. Some planned gifts do deliver cash in predictable amounts, and others support cash needs far into your organization's future.

Campaigns often run a number of years and therefore require a long-term planning horizon. A certain percentage of the planned gifts that are solicited during the course of a five- to six-year campaign will be realized (by the death of the donor) during that time frame. The marketing and interest generated by a campaign can also create a cash flow from bequests and other long-term gifts for years beyond the campaign time frame, which is clearly of benefit to the nonprofit. And, last but not least, some planned giving options work very well in producing current cash for current campaign needs.

Why Talk about Planned Giving?

- It can allow the donor to make a larger gift.
- It allows the donor to realize a tax advantage.
- It can increase retirement income.

- It fits well with raising endowment gifts.

- It can provide cash flow to your organization for years to come.

The marketing and use of planned gifts during a capital campaign depends on the expertise and staff available. All major gift officers, as well as lead volunteers, the director, and other key solicitors, should be trained in the basics of planned giving. Train your staff and volunteers to offer options when appropriate, but stop short of providing financial or legal advice to a donor; always tell the donor to consult with his or her own advisers to avoid legal issues and a conflict of interest.

Some campaigns market planned gifts heavily, selecting certain tools to encourage donors to give in ways that are helpful to the needs of that organization. Campaigns that include an endowment component, for instance, may wish to focus on bequest and life insurance gifts through mailings, advertisements, newsletters, and stories about donors. Many nonprofits set up donor recognition societies for planned giving donors so that they can achieve recognition and thanks before the gift is realized at their death.

Basic Types of Planned Gifts:

- Bequests

- Life insurance

- Retirement plans

- Life income plans
  - Charitable remainder trusts
  - Charitable gift annuities

- Charitable lead trusts

- Securities (stocks, bonds)

- Real estate

RULES OF THE ROAD

Never accept a gift that eats.

There are several types of planned gifts that can produce cash in the near future to meet the needs of a capital campaign:

Stock gifts can be sold right away and provide cash for capital projects. Most organizations set a policy that gifts of stock should not be held and should be sold right away. While some financial officers choose to hold stock in the interest of playing the market, issues of conflict of interest can arise, and the stock given may not match the portfolio needs and long-term investment policies of the nonprofit. All volunteers and development officers should have a cheatsheet that informs them of the policies for transfer and acceptance of stock gifts. These gifts are easy for the donor to understand and should be easy for the organization to execute.

Real estate gifts can be more complicated and take longer to turn into cash, but they are still attractive to the nonprofit and easy for the donor to understand. Because of the past decade's run-up in real estate values, this type of gift can produce a tax advantage for the donor, who avoids paying capital gains on the appreciation by giving away appreciated property. The nonprofit should have a policy for review of real estate gifts before acceptance, in order to avoid properties with liens, environmental hazards, joint ownership, or other legal problems.

The charitable lead trust allows the donor to pass along assets through a trust to her heirs at a substantial savings in taxes, while paying income for a set number of years to the nonprofit. Receiving money from a charitable lead trust is just like getting payments on a pledge, only the payments are guaranteed by the trust; as long as the assets in the trust maintain their value (i.e., there is no stock market crash), there is little risk to the organization. Setting up a lead trust requires that the donor obtain expert legal advice and is better suited to large gifts of $1 million and more, but it can be an excellent way to fund a gift to a capital campaign. From the organization's perspective, the lead trust provides a cash flow it can bank on for a guaranteed number of years.

Other planned gifts provide funds for the nonprofit over the longer term, usually upon the death of the donor. Campaigns that raise funds for endowments should definitely consider marketing planned giving tools as part of their fundraising plan. There is a very strong correlation between the thinking of a planned giving donor, who is looking at the long-term implications of his philanthropic giving, and the need of the organization for endowment, which is a long term method of providing ongoing support. Most large endowments in the United States have been built through major bequests; bequests have supported the founding of many of our most prominent universities.

Life income plans, such as charitable gift annuities and charitable remainder trusts, can be very attractive for building the organization's endowment. Life income plans are gifts that pay out income to a beneficiary for a lifetime or a set number of years. Because of their structure they don't produce immediate cash for the nonprofit. These giving vehicles, which normally pay income to a couple, a surviving spouse, or other beneficiary for a lifetime, give the remaining assets to the nonprofit when the term is up or the beneficiary passes away.

Bequests and life insurance gifts are also very appropriate for giving endowed funds to support the long-term financial health of the organization, even if they aren't realized for years. Making gifts through bequests is easy to understand but requires having a will. The donor can add a codicil to a will that is already in place. Recent research shows that less than half of Americans have wills, so a focus on estate planning in your marketing may help your efforts on this front. Some organizations use attorneys or estate planning experts to conduct seminars for their planned giving prospects.

Giving through *IRAs, Keoghs, and other tax-deferred retirement accounts* is also easy for the donor, but is sometimes overlooked as a planned giving tool. No legal work is required, as the donor has only to change the name of the beneficiary on the account form. The advantage of giving through retirement accounts is that the money does not pass through probate and is not subject to taxes; therefore, the full amount of the gift comes to the charity faster.

Women as Planned Giving Donors

The use of planned giving can be a major factor in tapping the wealth of women donors. Women in their fifties, sixties, and seventies, the age range of most leadership donors to capital campaigns, know that statistically they are likely to outlive their husbands. They want to be confident that they will have adequate health care and be able to maintain their independent lifestyles for 20 to 30 years more. Because of a dread of running out of money, many women are reluctant to part with major income-producing assets early in the retirement years. The use of planned giving tools, from bequests to trusts and annuities, can play an important role in the giving arrangements for these donors.

Another planned giving alternative that can be attractive to women donors is the gift of residence with a retained life interest. This allows the donor to make a gift of her home but retain the right to live in the house until she dies. The owner can make a gift of the home to the organization and achieve the tax benefits of the gift while still living in the house. The nonprofit will not actually realize the value of the home until the donor passes away and they sell the property.

The Annual Fund in the Capital Campaign

Raising gifts for ongoing programs and operations at the same time you are running a capital campaign can be confusing to the donor and difficult to manage for the staff. Campaign advisers differ on the approach to take, but several of the more common solutions to the problem are described below. Which path your organization takes depends on the sophistication and preferences of your volunteers and advancement staff, and ultimately, on your donors and their attitudes about giving to your organization.

TIPS & TECHNIQUES

Create a Bequest Chair for Your Campaign:

- Identify a current donor who has made a bequest to your organization.

- Ask this person to serve as your bequest chair.

- Ask the chair to sign letters to other current donors encouraging them to make a bequest to your organization.

- Feature the chair in ads or newsletter stories about bequests.

- Ask the chair to accompany you on calls to prospects for planned gifts.

- Hold a planned giving society event for bequest donors and prospects.

- Ask the chair to give a brief endorsement of the program at the event.

The Challenge: How to Continue to Raise Funds
for Operations during a Capital Campaign

Solution A: Integrate Annual Fund and Campaign Fundraising. Define the annual fund as one component of the overall campaign. Let annual fund donors know that through their annual fund gifts, they are supporting the goals of the campaign. Market the campaign to all donors at all levels of giving, but for all gifts up to a certain level, say $10,000, tell donors they will be used for annual operations. Gifts above $10,000 will be used for capital purposes, such as construction. Naming gifts can still be offered for leadership donors.

Pros:

- It includes all donors at all giving levels in the campaign.
- It allows lower-level gifts to be used for operations where they are needed.
- It keeps naming recognition focused on higher-level gifts.
- It reduces donor confusion about gift uses, levels, and dual solicitations.

Cons:

- It raises issues of campaign recognition for lower-level donors.
- It pulls higher donors away from the annual fund.
- It may result in less total money raised on a recurring annual basis, because higher-level donors may give only once to the campaign.

Solution B: Separate Annual Fund and Campaign Fundraising. Define the annual fund as a completely separate fundraising program from the capital campaign. Ask all donors to give to both the campaign and the annual fund through separate solicitations. Market the two fundraising programs separately.

Pros:

- Donors have a choice about where and when to make their gifts.

- Donors respond separately to each campaign as they are motivated.

- It may result in more money raised because loyal donors will give twice: once to the annual fund (each year); once to the capital campaign (on the campaign timetable).

Cons:

- Donors get confused over competing solicitations; it may turn off donors.

- Recognition issues are more complex.

 TIPS & TECHNIQUES

Consider reserving specific groups in your prospect pool for ongoing annual fund solicitations during the campaign. Delete certain donor groups from your campaign solicitations and ask them only for general operating support on an annual basis. Examples of groups that can be reserved for the annual fund:

- Grateful patients at a hospital

- Annual members or donors below a certain level (i.e., $100)

- Donors who haven't given in several years

- Donors acquired through direct mail

- People who visit your Web site

- Visitors or other users of your services whose names you acquire

- Donors can get confused over pledge schedules, annual fund fiscal years, and campaign timetables.

Solution C: The Dual Ask. Define the annual fund and the campaign as separate funds, but make an annual fund ask one component of the campaign solicitation for donors who will be receiving a personal solicitation, so only one ask takes place.

Pros:

- It reduces confusion on the part of donors.

- Those who are solicited personally have a volunteer or staff member there to explain all the needs of the organization.

- More money may be raised because the donor is giving to both funds.

- It keeps larger donors involved in the annual fund even while they are making pledges to the capital campaign.

- It allows the institution to keep its annual fund levels relatively stable during a campaign.

Cons:

- It requires training on the part of the volunteers and staff making the calls.

- It can be annoying to the donor, who is asked for two gifts at the same time.

- It can seem like nickel-and-diming a major donor to ask for annual fund on top of a large campaign gift.

- This is not an appropriate method for approaching corporations and foundations.

New Trends

Changes in Corporate and Foundation Giving

Corporate giving has gone through a major transformation in recent years, due to economic pressures, consolidation of smaller family-owned businesses into large public companies, and changes in accounting rules that now consider pledges as liabilities. These changes have resulted in a variety of new behaviors on the part of corporate gift makers.

First, fewer multiyear pledges are being made. Some corporations have stopped making pledges altogether and just make gifts from their annual giving budget. This can be problematic in a campaign, where donors in the past have used multiyear pledges to bring the total gift level up to a higher amount.

Another trend in corporate giving is the use of marketing budgets for naming rights, sponsorships, and gift making. For many companies, charitable giving has moved away from its roots in philanthropy. Now their goal is to attach the company's name to the best potential source of marketing outcomes. The "gift" thus becomes a marketing strategy to align the company's image with the nonprofit's clientele or mission.

Advertising tie-ins and sponsorships at charitable events are one common example of this development. As a result of the shift in corporate attitudes toward giving, some nonprofits now create contractual agreements with corporations for the terms under which a name will be carried, just like a sports arena would do. The corporate gift is rapidly being transformed into the corporate contractual obligation.

 RULES OF THE ROAD

Planned giving prospects: predeath individuals.

TIPS & TECHNIQUES

How to Market Endowment as Part of the Capital Campaign:

- Create a list of endowment naming opportunities and price levels.

- Focus on endowment giving when marketing planned gifts.

- Create a pooled endowed fund that is marketed to small donors.

- Identify the level of giving required to name a separate endowed fund (recommended minimum: $10,000 or $25,000).

- Train all volunteers and staff in the basics of endowment giving.

- Include endowment options in all campaign materials.

- Feature endowment donors and the projects their endowments have funded in ads and newsletters.

- Compare the size of your organization's endowment with that of your peers to help build the case for your needs.

Foundation giving has also been affected by changes in the external environment. Two or three years of stock market losses have hurt the ability of many foundations to take on the funding of new projects, and many have substantially reduced the amount of grant money they award annually. Some foundations are making gifts only to fund pledges they have outstanding. It will take several years of gains in the stock market to see this tendency turn around.

Foundations are also exhibiting an enhanced sense of global needs beyond the United States. Some foundations have begun to focus on giving grants that meet broad global goals, such as improving public health, providing educational opportunities to impoverished youth, or curing AIDS. Corporate foundations are responding to the fact that corporate profits are increasingly being earned from international markets, and global investors expect global philanthropy.

Finally, many foundations have become less willing to fund capital campaigns. Perhaps due to an increased focus on accountability and outcomes, foundations prefer to fund programmatic initiatives as opposed to bricks and mortar. There is also a strong reluctance to fund endowments because foundations themselves function as a kind of endowment, investing their principal and spending only the interest (usually 5%) on annual grants.

All of these changes in corporate and foundation giving make planning for the capital campaign more complex and more challenging. You must become aware of the giving attitudes and trends for the corporations and foundations most likely to support your organization.

Planning for Future Needs

Endowment Fundraising in the Capital Campaign

Many capital campaigns include both a capital and an endowment component. Whether your organization will be successful doing so depends on several factors.

First, consider the readiness of your organization to take on the management of an endowment. There are numerous policies and procedures you will need to have in place (see Exhibit 8.1). If your organization is cash-strapped and money for current needs is absolutely critical, this might not be the best time to start a savings account and salt away substantial sums against future needs.

You must also have donors who are sophisticated enough to understand the need for endowment. Some donors love the concept that the organization is saving the principal of their gift and spending only the interest. Others feel that endowments don't have enough bang for the buck; with annual expenditures of only 5% or so, an endowed gift does not have the same immediate impact on an organization as a fully expendable gift does.

EXHIBIT 8.1

Policies and Procedures Needed to Establish and Manage an Endowment

1. Minimum gift level to establish a named, restricted endowed fund

2. Benefits and recognition endowment donors will receive

3. Gift acceptance policy (What restricted uses and types of gifts will be accepted for an endowed fund?)

4. Investment policy (a formal, written document outlining the investment objective, goals, and guidelines for a portfolio; guides the investment planning process)

5. Payout policies (How much is going to be taken out each year? How will the payout be determined on an ongoing basis?)

6. Governance issues:
   - Determine whether you will use your finance committee or set up an investment committee to manage the endowment;
   - Decide what committee will have authority over decisions to accept restricted gifts and certain types of gifts.

Should Your Capital Campaign Include an Endowment Component?

Pros:

- It helps pay to keep the new facility open, operating, staffed, and maintained.

- It can be marketed as meeting long-term needs beyond the capital campaign.

- Some donors (mainly individuals) are interested only in giving to endowment.

- It may help to raise more money in total for the organization.

- It shows donors that the organization is planning for the long term, not just for immediate needs.

Cons:

- Donors can get confused between endowment and capital needs.

- It can be difficult to market both long-term and short-term needs.

- Endowment gifts are usually recognized in a different manner than capital gifts, which can be confusing to donors.

- The nonprofit has to be fiscally mature to plan for the investment, payout, accounting, and stewardship requirements that come with an endowment.

Publicize Outcomes

Because a capital campaign often results in visible additions to your organization's program, facilities, and offerings, the end of the campaign is a good time to publicize the outcomes. Most media outlets look for some kind of hook on which to base a story about your campaign successes. Events such as dedications, volunteer thank-yous, and the opening of new buildings can be attractive focal points for a local social or news column.

Ways to Attract Media Attention for a Capital Campaign Story:

- *Human interest:* Do a volunteer profile with interview.

- *Social:* Have a closing event, dedication ceremony, or groundbreaking event.

- *Business:* Profile a leadership donor who is a CEO or entrepreneur.

- *Architecture:* Interview the facility's architect.

- *Architecture:* Review unusual architectural details or environmentally friendly building components.

- *Social pages:* Create an award for outstanding service to your organization and give it to your campaign co-chairs.

- *Education:* Profile a student or teacher who uses the new program or facility.

- *Human interest:* Profile an unusual beneficiary or user of your program.

- *Business:* Create a financial report on the campaign, with number of donors, dollars raised, average gift, and economic impact of the project on the community.

- *Op ed:* Highlight the role of private giving in a time when government grants and public spending on the arts (or health care, or education) is waning.

- *Op ed:* Write about the role your organization is playing in providing services for underserved populations at a time when government funding is being cut.

- *Op ed:* Write about the role your organization is playing in expanding economic opportunity in your region.

Another way to publicize campaign results is to prepare a stewardship report for all campaign donors. This can take the form of an annual report, including donor recognition lists, or it can be a newsletter that illustrates outcomes, like the dedication of a new building. Some stewardship reports will need to be individualized. Foundation donors, for instance, often require reports that track the expenditure of funds that they provided and a report on programs funded.

Using the campaign to highlight the successes of your organization is one way in which you can reposition your nonprofit at the end of the campaign.

Enhanced public recognition of the results of your campaign will lead to more annual support and better opportunities for future special project funding, open doors to new avenues in your community, and ultimately strengthen your organization in the long term.

Closing the Campaign

There are a variety of ways to close a campaign, and the lines between shutting down one campaign and starting the next have begun to blur in many organizations. Some nonprofits have moved to a perpetual campaign mode, which can be exhausting for staff and volunteers, and most of all for donors. Other organizations take a more aggressive stance toward raising major gifts between campaigns in order to keep up fundraising totals.

The last months of the campaign offer some special opportunities for donor stewardship, recognition, and communication. It is especially important to make sure that your donors understand and approve of the details of the recognition you are offering them. Don't wait until the signs are literally set in stone to find out that your lead donor wants the building named for his mother, not himself.

Sample Timeline for the Last Year of the Campaign:

Six months before the end of the campaign:
- Plan dedications, groundbreakings, and other major events for new facilities.
- Secure approval *in writing* from all campaign donors on how they want their name to read for recognition purposes.
- Develop signage, create mockups of all major space signage, and get donor approval.
- Meet with donors who haven't selected naming spaces yet to determine recognition.

- Double check that you have written pledges on file for all campaign gifts.

Three months before the end of the campaign:
- Finalize plans for written recognition of donors such as campaign reports.
- Prepare lists for donor walls or other public recognition opportunities.
- Organize stewardship responsibilities among staff by project, level, or program.
- Prepare pledge reminder system; some major donors may require special handling of pledge payments.
- Clean up donor records and gift files.

At the end of the campaign:
- Prepare and distribute news media releases and campaign financial report.
- Print donor recognition lists.
- Thank volunteers and key campaign staff.
- Hold dedication or other celebratory event.
- Put up signage and donor walls.

Postcampaign:
- Send out pledge reminders.
- Track pledges in arrears and make calls on donors lagging in payments.
- Prepare stewardship reports to foundations.
- Prepare stewardship reports for endowment donors.
- Refocus fundraising efforts on annual operating funds.

Special Note to Advancement Staff at the End of the Campaign. The excitement is over quickly. Staff paid for on the campaign budget are often thanked one day and let go the next. Sometimes funds are budgeted to keep selected campaigners on staff beyond the campaign timetable, especially if the cash-flow level of a campaign can be maintained in the postcampaign period with an aggressive major gifts program.

But for many of those who see their first campaign through to the end, the final advice is: polish your resume. You are now an experienced campaigner. You are worth a lot to any organization! Move on, move up, or put your newly enhanced skills to work for another valuable nonprofit.

Index